LIZ CARTER is the author and translator of numerous Chinese-language textbooks and the co-author of *The Grass-Mud Horse Lexicon: Classic Netizen Language* (2013), which explores subversive Chinese internet culture. Formerly the managing editor of the website *Tea Leaf Nation*, she has appeared on Al Jazeera and HuffPost Live as an expert on youth culture in China. After working as a translator in Beijing, where she studied contemporary Chinese literature at Peking University, she relocated to Washington DC, where she works as a Chinese–English translator and writer.

"It is impossible to understand today's China without exploring how its internet users are transforming the country. Liz Carter blends smart analysis and colorful details to provide a glimpse into this fascinating world. *Let 100 Voices Speak* is a valuable contribution to the literature on the internet in China."

EMILY PARKER, author of
Now I Know Who My Comrades Are:
Voices From the Internet Underground

Let 100 Voices Speak

How the Internet is Transforming China and Changing Everything

LIZ CARTER

I.B. TAURIS

LONDON · NEW YORK

www.ibtauris.com

Published in 2015 by
I.B.Tauris & Co. Ltd
London • New York
www.ibtauris.com

ISBN: 978 1 78076 985 1
eISBN: 978 0 85773 921 6

A full CIP record for this book is available from the British Library
A full CIP record is available from the Library of Congress

Library of Congress Catalog Card Number: available

Illustrations copyright © Rose Adders
www.rossadams.co.uk

Text designed and typeset by Tetragon, London
Printed and bound by Page Bros, Norwich

Contents

Introduction

Thirty-five years ago, China's position on the world stage was peripheral, its population largely rural, its economy small, and its attention turned inward. After a decade-long Cultural Revolution that saw bitter ideological battles and the virtual suspension of formal education, the Chinese were just beginning to pick up the pieces. Today, China is the world's most populous country, as well as the world's second-largest and fastest-growing economy. More than half of all Chinese live in urban areas, and more than 600 million are internet users.

China is not rising; it has already risen. We still speak of an awakening or rising China because perceptions of the country were shaped decades ago, during its initial recovery, or even earlier, during its long period of political upheaval. Panicked by the idea that this long-held assumption has become invalid, observers have hastily sought to explain China, painting it as either a threat or a savior, 1 billion foreigners poised to redeem or destroy us all.

In truth, neither narrative is realistic. Some of what the Chinese economy does will benefit other world economies, and some of it may hurt. Some of the country's political moves may be welcome changes, and others more unpleasant. The idea that China will either save or destroy is based on two curious assumptions: first, that China has power to decide our fates, and that it will do so from its position entirely outside the West; and second, that there is a singular entity called China acting in a uniform manner based on unanimous consent.

What China is actually doing, and will continue to do, is changing us and being changed by us, until one day rhetoric catches up to reality and we no longer speak of China in terms of "us" and "them." Chinese products are exported throughout the world, China sends more students abroad than any other country, and the Chinese diaspora is one of the largest in history. Already, such overlap undermines the idea of China as an isolated entity. Changes in China, then, are not confined within the borders of the People's Republic.

Some of China's most dramatic changes are not occurring within its physical territory, but the somewhat more international space of the internet. Internet access first came to China in 1987, when researchers in Beijing sent an email to Germany, writing: "Across the Great Wall we can reach every corner in the world." Yet the most significant changes have happened more recently: For decades, the internet was used by only a tiny sub-segment of the world's most populated country, a tool for government researchers, professors, and technical experts. It was not until 2006 that China's internet penetration exceeded 10 percent.[1]

Since then, China's internet penetration has jumped to 46.9 percent (632 million users), double what it was ten years prior and still growing.[2] While Chinese internet penetration is lower than in most developed countries, there are roughly twice as many Chinese web users than there are people in the United States. If Chinese netizens formed a sovereign country, it would be the world's third largest.

Yet the most fascinating and significant aspect of the Chinese internet is not the number of people that have used it, but the uses it has served. Not only do China's internet users outnumber those of any other country, they are also far more social than their international counterparts. In 2012, 91 percent of Chinese internet users reported using social-media sites, compared to only 67 percent of US internet users.[3]

It is in China's social-media sphere that the battles and negotiations of change are taking place. Though the Chinese government blocked major foreign social-media sites like Facebook, YouTube, and Twitter in 2008 and 2009, Chinese companies have developed their own substitutes, often modeling them on their Western counterparts: Renren has been called the Chinese Facebook, Youku the Chinese YouTube, and Weibo the Chinese Twitter. These native sites have flourished by accommodating government censorship and surveillance demands as well as users' desire for a platform to connect and share content freely. While market demands push the companies to allow as much expression as possible, government requirements limit their ability to do so. The compromise that results is a line blurred by its constant, rapid movement, as social-media users – and companies – push the envelope and the government pushes back.

From 2011 to 2013, the majority of China's social web surfers used Weibo, a microblogging site often likened to Twitter. Like Twitter and Facebook, Weibo has been a game-changer. First of all, it's fast: In just an hour or two, a post can reach hundreds of thousands, if not millions, of people. Weibo also allowed for greater creativity and expression, because individuals were not subject to the same logistical and legal restrictions as in traditional media organizations. This is especially true in China, where the government regulates traditional media, like television, radio, and print newspapers, even more strictly than online social platforms.

This new virtual space has allowed outsiders to gain a broader, more nuanced understanding of China and has also given Chinese unprecedented space to create, connect, and challenge norms. With increased opportunities for connection across borders, the internet has helped erode long-standing prejudices. With increased opportunity for connection within China, it has facilitated community-building and information-sharing that will have an impact for years to come. The potential impact of these grass-roots, foundational shifts of assumptions and expectations cannot be overstated.

These struggles and shifts have opened up a space where activists can promote causes, and where artists and musicians can experiment and create. Social media has become a channel for expression that is less effectively censored than established institutions like publishing houses and the film industry. The internet, as the great equalizer, has also lowered economic barriers to entry for entrepreneurs, activists, and ordinary people looking to talk and connect. It has fostered communities of ideas that have grown large enough to compete with communities of privilege.

Censors have kept pace with the internet's developments, adapting with new technologies and techniques. Most recently, Chinese authorities have even weaponized internet traffic to carry out censorship beyond China's borders, using what has become known as the "Great Cannon" to execute distributed denial-of-service (DDoS) attacks on domains hosted abroad. But China's censorship is not an all-or-nothing matter. There are many different shades and degrees: Censorship is implemented in a variety of ways and for a variety of purposes. At times, attempts to block the spread of information have backfired, and, most importantly, information control has shaped the very way that Chinese speak and write their own language. The complexity of China's censorship has forced China's internet users to respond in equally complex ways; in China, censorship has fueled creativity.

While the government has done a remarkable job of using its knowledge and control of social media to maintain stability, these are largely short-term successes. Targeted censorship of posts that call for collective action may have prevented dissatisfaction on social media from translating directly into real-world action in some cases, as the response to such cases has shown that protests may be defused, but less attention has been paid to the slow, subtle changes that Weibo has brought about in Chinese society. Routine appeasement of social-media users has built up expectations among China's citizens that they can force authorities to change, making China's an adaptive authoritarian government. As Jon Sullivan wrote, Weibo's role in forcing the government's hand in specific crises may not be as important as its less publicized role in "a longer term process by which netizens become accustomed to greater transparency, political participation, and demand more systematic mechanisms for accountability."[4]

Weibo and other social-media platforms are windows into these lesser-noted, large-scale shifts: A mother tirelessly seeks justice for her 11-year-old daughter, who was held in a brothel and raped for months, and in the process inspires a change in Chinese law. A daughter demands justice after her father's hurried execution, sparking a national conversation about China's judicial system. Millions of young Chinese, facing the rising rate of unemployment and sky-high property prices, begin to push back against societal expectations of compliance and conformity. This book is about their stories.

one

COVER-UPS
AND
UNCOVERINGS

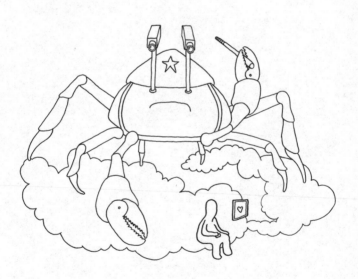

I t began with a crash.

On July 23, 2011, two high-speed trains were moving along the "Harmony Express," a north–south line that follows China's coast. The trains were carrying passengers south through Zhejiang province, one of China's wealthiest, to the city of Fuzhou. A number of those on board were young students taking the train south to start summer internships. Others were en route to visit family, some traveling with relatives and others riding alone, passing the time until their reunions by reading books or watching movies. It was ten o'clock at night: The sun had set hours before, and rain pelted the windows of the sleek, new train cars.

A lightning storm had already damaged part of the track that Saturday evening. The first train, carrying more than 1,000 people, had stopped on a viaduct after encountering a signaling issue; the second, carrying 558 people at more than 100 miles per hour, received the go-ahead to continue moving – and crashed into the rear of the first. Four railway cars plummeted 50 feet from the top of the viaduct to the ground below.

The impact of the two trains colliding and its aftermath killed 40 people and injured nearly 200 more. A Chinese American man visiting the country with his parents lost both mother and father, and sustained severe injuries of his own. One man lost not only his wife – pregnant with their unborn child – but her mother and sister, and his niece. A toddler was rescued from the crash – but her mother and father both perished in it. This was not only the first high-speed rail accident to cause fatalities in China, but the third deadliest in human history.

China's government immediately reacted – by attempting to control bad press. Propaganda authorities ordered news outlets not to link to previous articles on high-speed-rail development or publish "reflective" articles – presumably, those that would explore the larger causes of the accident. "Do not investigate the causes of the accident," one order issued to media outlets read. "Use information released from authorities as standard [...] Do not question. Do not elaborate. No re-posting on microblogs will be allowed!"[1]

In another country, perhaps, concerned citizens might have turned on their televisions and watched live coverage by CNN or the BBC, but this was impossible in China, where such live coverage is extremely rare and heavily restricted. Officials there use their considerable power to shape the public's understanding of events like the Wenzhou train crash, and press gags are commonplace. In an earlier age, papers across the country might have played down the story and lowered the death toll, relegating the news of the crash to the inner pages or choosing not to print it altogether. But, on that night in 2011, something was different. Even before morning papers came out the next day, many Chinese had learned about the collision.

That night, millions had powered up their computers and smartphones, hoping to learn about what was happening in Wenzhou. It was primarily on Weibo, a new social-media site, that those hungry for news found up-to-the-minute, even up-to-the-second information about the crash. Weibo users quickly gathered information about those missing, injured, and dead, numbers consistently higher than those announced by the government. Even Chinese state-run media agreed that Weibo was the "first source of information" about the accident and that it played a very important role in recovery efforts.[2]

The fact that information was spreading through social media would have been nothing more than a footnote in the history of the Wenzhou crash, but, very quickly, it became a significant aspect of the story. Instead of merely supplementing coverage by state-run media, social media was supplanting it. Instead of adding detail to the in-depth reporting by China's sanctioned traditional news media, Weibo users were doing the heavy lifting, even going so far as to challenge directly official versions of events and demand that authorities dig deeper to find the responsible parties. As the *New York Times* wrote, not long after the crash: "This week's performance may signal the arrival of weibos as a social force to be reckoned with."[3]

Weibo posts about the crash and its aftermath exceeded 10 million in just one week, with the vast majority criticizing the government's handling of the situation.[4] Truthfully, there was much to criticize. Heavily invested in preserving the image of the rail system – which is state-owned and operated in China – authorities seemed to be trying to contain the story, rather than attempting to get to the bottom of it. The numerous missteps made by various branches of the government throughout the recovery efforts only provoked more anger from the public.

Weibo users were perhaps most opposed to the move to bury some of the wreckage – seen by most as a literal cover-up. Images of heavy machinery chopping up parts of the wreckage and burying them began to circulate online just 48 hours after the accident occurred. Workers from the railways ministry succeeded in burying one car before a Weibo-fueled backlash forced them to unearth it. In one Weibo poll, which asked, "Which reason do you believe for why the train was buried?" 98 percent of the more than 60,000 respondents selected the option "Destruction of evidence."[5]

Official attempts to censor and guide media coverage also angered readers. But even employees of state-owned news agencies in China balked at the orders, usually observed carefully to avoid retaliation, posting information in real time via their personal Weibo accounts.[6]

Weibo also made immediate contributions to recovery efforts, as users pushed back against the official death toll and crowdsourced information about how ordinary people could help. In response to an appeal posted on Weibo for people in the area to donate blood, more than 1,000 showed up to the donation center in a line that stretched to the door.[7] But equally impressive were the underlying changes in public expectations of transparency and accountability that users of the site made clear as they rallied to demand explanations and justice. Weibo users' reaction to the crash and its handling revealed the power concentrated on the platform and in each user. The backlash against censorship was also unprecedented, revealing limits to the government's ability to curb and contain groundswells of dissent online.

When workers began to bury the wreckage, it was the outcry on Weibo that stopped them. When the local judicial bureau forbade lawyers from accepting cases from victims – citing the sensitivity of the issue – it was the Weibo backlash that forced them to recant and apologize. Weibo users prodded and questioned at every stage of the recovery and investigation, forcing an in-depth look at the accident that ultimately found 54 officials accountable to various degrees and forced a massive scaling back of the country's high-speed rail, which had long been touted as symbolic of the Party's commitment to rapid development and innovation.

The Wenzhou train crash, which would become one of the biggest news stories of 2011, had implications for ordinary Chinese men and women beyond even the tragic death toll. Travel by train is one of the main means of transportation in China, and more than a billion trips are taken by rail there each year.[8] Often, there are few other choices: Most Chinese don't own cars, and air travel is prohibitively expensive for many. That such a huge collision had taken place between two of China's most modern trains, in one of the wealthiest parts of the country, had the potential to raise concern about the rate of China's development.

After Wenzhou, Weibo acted as an equalizer: The rapid transmission of information allowed the platform to compete with, and at times successfully defeat, the traditional media, which was more firmly under government control. In that sense it was a platform for the people to resist what they felt was unfair treatment by the government.

This new status quo, while heartening to those hungry for information in the aftermath of events like Wenzhou, was threatening to China's government. Officials afraid of any change at all – let alone rapid transformation – were terrified that a newly founded social-media site could supplant the state-run papers that had controlled the narrative for decades. After the trains collided, it became clear that Weibo wasn't another internet time-suck for bored teenagers, but a dangerous and unpredictable force that could change absolutely everything.

What is Weibo? Literally translated, the name means "microblog" – it is a social-media website that allows users to publish 140-character posts that will then appear in the feeds of their followers, much like Twitter.[9] Popular among younger, tech-savvy Chinese and the urban middle class, Weibo had been around for about a year at the time of the Wenzhou crash, but already it had more than 140 million users, many of them very active.

Blogging has long been popular in China, but microblogging took the dissemination of information to another level. A Chinese web user who once had to visit a number of blogs to keep up with their topics of interest could use Weibo to scroll through their carefully tailored timeline, or search for content and accounts related to new interests. With Weibo, control shifted from the content creator to the content consumer, a change that appealed to the world's second-largest economy. At its peak, Weibo boasted more than 500 million registered users, of whom 54 million used the site daily.

With hundreds of millions of people constantly posting on the site and refreshing to see new content, Weibo had the potential to become an unstoppable force. And after Wenzhou, it seemed that the outcry on Weibo had become loud enough to rival mainstream media, official statements, and the Party line. The backlash, and its handling, marked the beginning of a tumultuous period in China, one in which social media began to transform public debate.

What disasters reveal

The reaction to the Wenzhou crash was astonishing, but it had its roots in how web users had followed another disaster three years earlier – the 2008 Sichuan earthquake. The

8.0-magnitude quake, which struck central China in May of that year, left tens of thousands dead and at least 4.8 million homeless.[10] It ripped the countryside apart and was felt in cities more than 1,000 miles away. East of the epicenter, workers evacuated their buildings in Shanghai. North of it, in Gansu province, the moving earth warped the rails on which a freight train was carrying more than a dozen tankers of gasoline; it derailed and burst into flames.[11]

This disaster – China's deadliest earthquake in decades – also laid bare a chilling reality: While government buildings remained standing in the aftermath, many schools throughout the affected area had crumbled to dust. They shouldn't have. Resources had been allocated to build strong, resilient schools (experts were aware that the area was at risk of earthquakes), but these funds had been siphoned off by everyone from the local officials in charge to the construction companies themselves, who cut corners every step of the way. In the end, the shoddy construction materials they used crushed countless children to death.

Disturbed by the needless loss of life, internationally renowned artist Ai Weiwei began to blog about disaster relief efforts and worked to collect the names and birthdays of all the students who had died – information that authorities refused to release themselves. Another activist, Tan Zuoren, investigated how the quake caused the collapse of school buildings, which became known as "tofu structures" for their flimsiness. Their efforts were met with harsh suppression. Censors took down Ai Weiwei's popular blog and placed him under surveillance, later confiscating his passport; Tan Zuoren was imprisoned for "incitement of subversion" and spent five years in jail.[12] It became clear that attempts to dig deeper into the corruption the quake had exposed would not be tolerated.

Despite these harsh measures – seemingly successful attempts by the government to control the narrative – the disaster changed China in a way that could not be undone. Critical voices, both online and off, persisted in spite of the danger, using every tool the internet could offer to expose corruption and address the problems in China's systems of power.

Grass-roots Weibo celebrities

The 2008 quake was also a turning point for a man who would go on to become one of China's most influential public intellectuals in the social-media era. Li Chengpeng, a sports journalist, called himself a "typical patriot" prior to the tragedy, blaming the West for China's problems and refusing to criticize the government.[13] But what he saw in the disaster-stricken area, where he had rushed to help victims of the earthquake, changed him forever: "It became clear that the 'imperialists' did not steal the reinforced-steel bars from the concrete used to make our schools," he wrote in an essay published on the fourth anniversary of the quake. "Our school children were not killed by foreign devils. Instead, they were killed by the filthy hands of my own people."[14]

Li spoke for a broad swath of Chinese society. Like many of China's urban middle class, he was born in the 1960s and entered the workforce in the 1980s, when the country's economy was just liberalizing. He made a name for himself as a sportswriter covering soccer, but became nationally known when he criticized the match-fixing and corruption in the China Football Association. In spite of the danger, Li spoke out about the issue numerous times during his career, even publishing a book about his findings.[15]

Concern over the corruption of China's soccer federation – which involved match-fixing and the bribery of referees – was another factor that drove Li to write about corruption in Chinese society at large. He followed the match-fixing scandals all the way to the top, and realized that the problems found in the state-run sports system could be seen in many other institutions.

Since his first foray into anti-corruption activism in 2008, Li has become quite popular, but it was joining Weibo that brought his blog posts to a wider audience. Li became one of the most outspoken voices on the platform, where he had more than 7.3 million followers.[16] Weibo users who otherwise would not visit a separate website to seek him out often saw his posts reposted by their friends and other celebrities. While Li had "only" 6 or 7 million followers, his posts frequently trended, which meant that almost all of the site's active users would have seen links to them from the site's main page.

Since he began to tackle corruption, Li has had a rough time with the authorities. He has been banned, fired, and censured, had his social-media account deleted, had his articles cut, and been threatened with violence – but the popular blogger defines himself by his willingness to keep going, acceding to authorities' individual demands when necessary, but continuing to test boundaries.

Weibo has made it possible for people like Li, who give voice to public dissatisfaction, to rise rapidly in prominence. Each viral post made by Li reached many Weibo users who might not have heard of him before. As he became more well known, he brought to his audience's attention the deeper problems apparent in times of crisis, inspiring yet more people to speak out about issues like corruption.

Over the years, Li continued to speak out on issues of corruption and government malfeasance, and the Wenzhou train crash was no exception: "This train was going too fast," he wrote of the accident. "Just like this country. It demands that we continuously engineer GDP miracles."[17] For Li, the fatal Wenzhou accident opened the door to discussions about the government's willingness to risk the lives of Chinese for intangible economic figures and international standing. And thanks to Weibo, Li's message spread, encouraging the millions concerned about the tragedy to consider its broader implications for China as a whole.

The human-flesh search—
how Weibo brought down the powerful

Weibo was powerful because of its speed – this became apparent as information spread rapidly after the Wenzhou train crash. It also proved able to empower brave individuals like Li Chengpeng, who were willing to speak out even after receiving death threats. Yet the main reason the site became a game-changer for China was not a courageous blogger or site feature, but its user base: hundreds of millions of people who knew they had strength in numbers.

A broad swath of anonymous users made Weibo a dynamic and volatile sphere. Less afraid of social backlash – and loosed from the sometimes constrictive ideas of proper behavior that permeate mainstream society in China – unnamed individuals pushed the envelope by posting on sensitive issues like government cover-ups and corruption cases. Their actions also inspired others to do and say what would otherwise be unthinkable.

Perhaps a single Weibo user might fear to post sensitive information – afraid of censorship, arrest, or even violent backlash – but together, millions of users could conduct a "human-flesh search," or *ren rou sousuo* in Chinese. This macabre-sounding activity involved such a broad distribution of tasks in a kind of crowdsourced stalking that it was difficult – though not impossible – to hold a single user responsible. For just this reason, it was the perfect weapon in the fight against official malfeasance.

Crowdsourcing the fight against government corruption

Before getting into the ways in which the human-flesh search has been a tool for fighting the good fight, it's important to note the ways in which it can be dangerous. In many instances, the speed with which the human-flesh search takes place and the fervor with which information has been pursued has resulted in cases of mistaken identity, or incredibly harsh punishment. The ease with which individuals can satisfy their desire for justice, or at the very least vengeance, can lead them to do terrible things.

In 2008, for instance, a student at Duke University in North Carolina named Grace Wang was subjected to a human-flesh search after she tried to promote discussion between opposing protest groups on campus: supporters of Tibetan independence, and Chinese who declared that Tibet was a part of China's sovereign territory. Pictures of Grace that showed her in front of the crowd supporting Tibetan independence circulated online – the angle of the camera did not capture the fact that she was positioned between the two opposing groups.

The viral pictures and human-flesh search that followed resulted in the vicious harassment of Grace Wang's family. Internet users posted their home address online, forcing her parents to flee from an influx of threatening messages. Someone even dumped a bucket of shit in front of their house in China. All of this was before Weibo, where what once took days might have taken minutes. Posts have gone from zero to more than 100,000 reposts in little more than an hour on Weibo: In 2012, Grace Wang's family might not have had time to run.

Clearly, a human-flesh search is not preferable to a working justice system, but for many ordinary Chinese, stonewalled by law enforcement and local-government cadres, it appears to be one of the only ways of addressing official corruption. Corruption is not just unpopular in China – it is also a trigger for many people there who experience it in their daily lives but have little recourse for their own grievances. The chance to see at least someone, somewhere punished is personally satisfying for the average Chinese web user.

From 2010 to 2014, Weibo-based human-flesh searches drew blood, taking down a number of people, mostly government officials or employees of state-owned enterprises. One thing that Chinese social media made abundantly clear is that nothing stays buried forever. Officials can keep affairs under wraps for only so long before a mistress posts an incriminating photo on Weibo, while a single slip-up in a padded business contract can leave an information trail for a web-savvy investigative journalist.

Take the example of Yang Dacai, known colloquially as "Watch Brother." Yang, the chief of the Shaanxi province Safety Supervision Bureau, was photographed smiling at the scene of an accident in which 36 people died on August 28, 2012. Enraged by his callous response, Weibo users reposted the picture, bringing him into the social-media spotlight. Others shared pictures taken over the years, in which Yang wore a number of expensive watches.[18] Still more internet users identified the various watches and their retail prices. Eventually, the crowdsourced evidence led to an investigation, which led to a trial. Just one year after the initial social-media snafu, Yang was sentenced to 14 years in prison for corruption.[19]

The evidence of official corruption is often out in the open. It is difficult to hide a luxury sedan or a Rolex watch – these are possessions people buy precisely in order to flaunt them. But in years past, officials felt at least a modicum of safety in their embezzlement because the locals who witnessed their extravagance were powerless to do anything about it. Either they were afraid of getting on the bad side of the powers that be, or they thought that local law-enforcement agencies would be in the pockets of these corrupt offenders.

In the age of the internet, such fears of retaliation are diminished: Residents of a Beijing suburb have little to fear from the mayor of a small town in southern Yunnan province. Furthermore, anonymity and the power of numbers online make it harder for authorities to find any single person to blame for exposing corruption. Perhaps most importantly, a large virtual campaign can collect enough incriminating evidence – and raise enough awareness – to make protecting these lower-level offenders a losing proposition for higher-level authorities.

In the fight against the government, there is a fight within the government

In most articles, lower- and higher-level authorities are lumped together into one group – "China's government" or "Chinese authorities" – but the distinction between them is a large part of what makes vigilante Weibo justice possible. Behind takedowns like that of Yang Dacai, a larger power struggle is taking place – not one between China's people and its government, but another between local authorities and central-government figures. Over the past two decades, national legislators have passed a number of laws quietly transferring the power to collect taxes and make budgets from local to central authorities, in effect moving in on their money and power.[20]

As the central government has far more control over the internet than local governments, it can use the web as a lever to gain even more control. It has access to the servers for all major Chinese sites, and directly controls ministries in charge of internet affairs. Central authorities can use the power of the internet to intimidate or sway lower-level officials and bodies, either by protecting local officials and ministries charged with corruption or by letting angry netizens have at them. In this ongoing struggle, the central government makes major short-term gains by allowing the Weibo-using public to ride roughshod over their "little tyrants."

Letting Yang and his Rolexes take the fall, for example – instead of ordering the censorship team at Sina, the media company that owns Weibo, to erase mention of him online – was a win–win scenario for China's central government and ordinary Chinese. Ordinary Chinese succeeded in bringing down a corrupt official, and the central government was able to appear responsive to the people while sending a message to other lower-level officials.

Online takedowns, like the toppling of Watch Brother, happened before Weibo, but they took a lot longer. The ability of microblogging to transmit information virally may have accelerated the whistle-blowing-to-response process. It took only 63 hours, for example, for a government official named Lei Zhengfu to be sacked after footage of him having sex was leaked online.[21] Lei, who was Communist Party secretary of a district in the megalopolis of Chongqing, was another corrupt official taken down by Weibo.

On November 20, 2012, the sex tape of Lei – a portly, middle-aged man whom the *New York Times* called "memorably unattractive" – in bed with a beautiful young woman in her teens or twenties went viral.[22] The five-year-old recording was originally intended as blackmail: It was said that Lei was so rich from corruption that real-estate developers could no longer afford to bribe him, so they had to find other ways to get leverage. The developers paid a number of young women to seduce him and recorded the evidence. But the attempt at blackmail didn't work out quite as planned. When developers tried to hold the recording over Lei's head in 2009, he reported them to the public-security authorities in Chongqing. Authorities detained the woman in question for a month, and jailed the developer.[23] But the video itself wasn't destroyed. Eventually, a source within the local public-security bureau handed it over to a grass-roots anti-corruption investigator called Zhu Ruifeng.

Zhu, who claims to have exposed more than 100 dirty officials and brought down a third of them, runs a site called People's Supervision.[24] But he had a little help bringing attention to the case of Lei. Weibo drove traffic to Zhu's site – as many as 20 million hits – after an investigative journalist named Ji Xuguang took to Weibo to post screenshots of the tape and links to the original clips on Zhu's site.[25]

Zhu said he felt as though in recent days something had "shifted": The reporting-to-removal process was much quicker.[26] He reported that, in past cases, his activities had ended in censorship and censure, but after uploading Lei's sex tape, he was informed that police had received instructions to protect him. The leaked tape had a domino effect: By early 2013, ten other government officials and executives of state-owned enterprises had fallen in related investigations.[27] Weibo, powered by its hundreds of millions of users, was able to force change in ways that were impossible before by making Zhu's whistleblowing too loud to ignore.

In 2012, it seemed that few weeks went by without news of a local official found to have amassed mountains of ill-gotten gains. There was Gong Aiai, a bank official in Shaanxi province, discovered to be in possession of 41 Beijing apartments. Shan Zengde, a deputy minister of agricultural development in Shandong province, came under fire after someone leaked a strangely incriminating document online: a promise to his mistress, signed and fingerprinted, to divorce his wife within one month.[28] *Baidu Baike*, China's answer to *Wikipedia*, even rolled out a special section devoted to "officials who have fallen under the horse," cataloging the rise and fall of government workers gone bad.[29]

These and other real-world results of Weibo activity are testament to the platform's arrival, just a few years after its founding, as a force to be reckoned with. The Wenzhou train crash demonstrated the power inherent in its speed and the ease with which information could spread. Li Chengpeng's rise to fame showed that Weibo would amplify the voices of those brave enough to criticize national policy. And the numerous corrupt officials exposed on the site by ordinary web users were living proof that some power – though not all – had found its way into the hands of the people. Weibo's speed and strength in numbers gave it a momentum that authorities were often unable to curb effectively.

If all of this sounds too good to be true, it's because these victories are only part of the larger picture. The rest of the story is in black and white as well as every shade in between: Buildings have burned, laws have changed, hundreds have been arrested and millennia-old cultural attitudes have begun to shift. But the tale of China's social internet cannot be told without first painting a clearer picture of the beast that inhabits that forest: state-sponsored censorship.

—two—

CENSORSHIP IS THE MOTHER OF SUBVERSION

Censorship sounds fairly straightforward, calling to mind redacted reports and banned books. But in China it is much more than the removal of words. It is a vast apparatus. Its bulk is both an asset and a weakness, hampering its ability to exercise total control over China's incredibly fast and agile web users while simultaneously scaring many into self-censorship by virtue of its sheer size. Like Walt Whitman, it contains multitudes, with the phrase "censorship authorities" referring to top government decision-making bodies, low-level employees of commercial media firms who spend their days deleting web posts, and millions of others besides.

The easiest way to deal with such a dauntingly complex subject would be to describe it in terms of the reasons it is bad. However, nothing about China will really make sense without a more refined understanding of state censorship. The following is an attempt to make sense of censorship as it exists in China: its characteristics, its origin story, how it is evolving, what people think about it, and how it sees itself. Most importantly, this chapter deals with the relationship between Chinese social-media users and censorship: the story of how repressive measures have had some remarkable unintended consequences.

But before we arrive at the end, let us start at the beginning, with a rough sketch of China's internet-censorship apparatus, in all its authoritarian glory.

Perhaps because Chinese authorities recognize the potential of the net as a threat as well as a tool, they have invested heavily in the "Great Firewall" and the "Golden Shield Project," sophisticated technological apparatuses that allow the government to censor unwanted content and websites, as well as monitor internet users' surfing activity and online communications.[1] A team of engineers – with assistance from US companies, many believe – began to develop the firewall in 1998 and spent eight years perfecting it. Though data on the project's costs is hard to come by, just one part of the project, the National Information Security Management System, cost $61 million to build.[2] Authorities are constantly updating and strengthening these systems.

China's government also budgets money for personnel – censorship is not an unmanned machine. Some members of the People's Liberation Army fill these roles; other slots go to computer science graduates or to people who just need a job. Increasingly, authorities have pushed the burden of censorship to private companies, but they cannot trust all sites to police content to levels they find satisfactory: Thus, the government foots the bill for an official internet army.

Publicly available data about the number of censors in China is lacking, but scattered information sheds some light on the profession. One Harvard study claimed that the government recommended that private sites hire two to three censors per 50,000 users. Sina Weibo claimed to have about 600 million registered users at its peak, but even assuming it required censors for only half that number, it would have needed to employ 24,000 to 36,000 people.[3] The popular mobile chat client WeChat, which employs its own censors, has just as many users. Even smaller social platforms can boast millions of active users, which means even more censors.

The very scale of public- and private-sector censorship is a testament to how powerful these platforms can be.

Over the past several years, authorities have passed a series of laws holding internet service providers, media outlets, and even individuals legally responsible for spreading illegal content. The definition of illegal content is also vague enough that courts could convict over virtually any statement authorities don't want online. Bloggers, journalists, activists, and ordinary people have been arrested, tried, sentenced, jailed, and sent to labor camps for statements that "incite subversion of state power," or cause "public disorder."

A lot of borderline-sensitive content escapes censorship, but authorities are also quite harsh, and seemingly arbitrary. As recently as 2010, Chinese police sent a woman to a labor camp for an entire year for a sarcastic tweet.[4] Internet users who make one too many controversial statements are summoned to "have tea" with authorities, and encouraged during these meetings to back down.

Making public examples of these individuals or groups of people is known in Chinese as "killing the chicken to scare the monkey." China scholar Perry Link famously described the specter of potential punishment as the anaconda in the chandelier: It need strike only occasionally; the "controlling power of fear" was what really got the job done.[5]

A more recent Harvard study on China's censorship found that Link's decade-old metaphor still held water: "Based on interviews with those involved in the process, we also find a great deal of uncertainty over the exact censorship requirements and the precise rules for which the government would interfere with the operation of social-media sites," wrote the researchers. "This uncertainty is in part a result of encouraging innovation, but it may also in some situations be a means of control as well – it being easier to keep people away from a fuzzy line than a clearly drawn one."[6]

Not everything is fuzzy. Chinese law explicitly requires internet service providers to maintain surveillance records of users and facilitate government surveillance, and it mandates that internet cafes collect the identification information of their patrons and report illegal activity. As internet use becomes far more mobile than before – the majority is now conducted on mobile devices, while internet use in cafes has dropped significantly – new laws and regulations continue to take aim at anonymity.

Since 2000, authorities have revised the bland-sounding "Internet Information Service Management Rules" by increments, requiring private-sector players to facilitate an increasing amount of censorship and surveillance.[7] Most of these revisions have taken place since 2011, when China established the State Internet Information Office to deal with its growing internet sector. In late 2012, China's legislature passed rules forcing "network service providers that handle website access services for users, handle fixed telephone, mobile telephone and other surfing formalities, or provide information publication services to users" to require users to provide their real identification information.[8] Knowledge of these trends further encourages self-censorship by social-media users as well as internal censorship by private-platform operators.

Many would argue that it could be worse: In 2009, China actually shut down the internet completely for several months in Xinjiang province, after ethnic riots there left hundreds dead.[9] But more subtle censorship has its own downsides. Less easy to see or detect, censorship that flies beneath the radar is also harder to fight. In 2013, for example, Weibo began to phase out the total blockage of certain terms in its search engine and phase in a more subtle form of censorship: the pruning of search results to give the illusion of unfettered access to information. Jason Ng, the author of a book on Chinese social media, *Blocked on Weibo*, saw the move as a step backward in some ways: "Whether full-scale or piecemeal, the reduction of blanket keyword blocks is paradoxically a loss of transparency, since Chinese users no longer explicitly know when certain results are being specifically targeted for censorship," he wrote in an article for the website *Tea Leaf Nation*. "What is and is not off-limits has now become slightly harder to determine – another step in making censorship invisible and all-pervasive."[10]

A look to the past

Chinese social media suffers from a vast array of restrictions, flavors of censorship most outside the country have never tasted. On the surface, the scope and scale of state-sponsored censorship brings to mind the dystopian world of George Orwell's *Nineteen Eighty-four*, where the government controls the press and Big Brother is always watching. Yet censorship is less effective today than it once was. Today's censorship is an entirely different animal than it was in China's not-so-distant past.

Much of today's censorship has roots in the political career of Mao Zedong, the leader who dominated the People's Republic of China from its founding in 1949 to his death in 1976. Despite paying lip service to freedom of speech and the importance of not shooting the messenger, Mao was known for persecuting those whose words he disliked.

In particular, Mao's policies during the Cultural Revolution, which lasted from 1966 to 1976, created a foundation for modern Chinese censorship. The Cultural Revolution was a period of intense propaganda and censorship in which the Party strictly controlled the news and entertainment sectors to ensure ideological purity. It also banned most foreign books, movies, and music. Because censorship was incorporated into the publishing process, authorities were able to control the final content that was distributed nationwide fairly effectively. Certain materials slipped through the cracks, but these instances were the exception, not the rule.

Mao's death in 1976 was followed by the end of the Cultural Revolution and widespread fatigue from endless censorship, propaganda, and economic stagnation. Deng Xiaoping and other top officials regained power and began to push through a series of economic and political reforms in 1978 – though more of the former than the latter. Private business, illegal for decades, was allowed and even encouraged through preferential policies and the establishment of special economic zones. This program was known as the "Reform and Opening." Economic liberalization, organizational reform, and the welcoming of foreign investment spurred China's recovery.

As the private sector developed, Chinese society changed dramatically. Ideology took a backseat to practicality; political correctness became less a matter of life and death and more perfunctory posturing. These changes, combined with increasing contact with the world outside China, made a wealth of information available once more to ordinary Chinese citizens.

The government continued to restrict the media, but as it withdrew funding for newspapers and magazines, these media outlets had to strike an increasingly difficult balance. Appeasing government censors kept them in business, but meeting readers' demands for real news paid their bills. Furthermore, Chinese-language media outlets based in Taiwan and Hong Kong also began to expand into mainland China. These organizations, based in areas with far greater freedom of speech, competed with mainland-Chinese papers for readership, forcing China's domestic media to adapt.

China has liberalized over the past several decades, and traditional methods of censorship have adapted to keep pace with rapid, large-scale changes in Chinese society. But the development and popularization of the internet have made it even more difficult for authorities to control public opinion through content censorship or propaganda. By dispersing the tools for information dissemination to ordinary citizens, the internet decentralized reporting, and thus made the task of enforcing censorship prior to dissemination all but impossible.

Online, censorship remains a factor, but it occurs after content is published, not before. Weibo and other social-media platforms have turned over control of publication to the people, and the increase in power has made pre-emptive censorship infinitely more difficult. Now, much of the burden of censorship falls on human censors, who must scan a great amount of content and delete unwanted posts by hand. Government censorship, which was once a matter of central planning, now closely resembles crisis control.

What about Weibo?

Weibo arrived on the scene just a few years ago, a censored social-media platform in a censored environment. It was thought by many to be a playground of sorts, a contained space that would amuse and distract China's hundreds of millions of web users. It undoubtedly sold itself as such to Chinese authorities: otherwise it would have met the same fate as its many predecessors.

In previous pushes to control the online world, Chinese authorities have shuttered whole operations. Before Weibo, there was Twitter, which was starting to take off in China when it was blocked in June 2009, just before the anniversary of the Tiananmen Square crackdown.[11] Though it continues to operate – and many Chinese still use it via censorship circumvention technology – web users based in mainland China who type twitter.com into their browsers are informed that "This webpage is not available." Domestic precursors to Weibo, Jiwai and Fanfou, got the ax following a series of ethnic riots in western China that left hundreds dead and injured in July 2009. Facebook was also blocked at this time, as authorities scrambled to control media coverage of the unrest.[12]

For a while, Chinese simply used the social networks they had before microblogging became the order of the day. Forums have always been popular in China, and they continued to support large online communities. But everyone in the internet business, both in China and outside the country, had already seen the market potential for microblogging in the short time that it had been allowed to flourish. Even with the ax of censorship looming overhead, the opportunity was too good to pass up.

The company in the right place at the right time was Sina, a massive new-media enterprise that dominated the online news and entertainment market. Charles Chao, then a rising star at Sina, ordered the launch of a microblogging platform to fill the void left by the blocking of Twitter and its imitators. Chao, like many of Sina's top executives, was US-educated (in accounting and journalism) but had returned to his home country, drawn by the opportunities of a market growing by leaps and bounds.

In August 2009, Sina launched Weibo, which has been the top microblogging platform in China ever since. While other platforms have been shut down, Charles Chao's alleged close ties to the son of Hu Jintao, who served as president of China for ten years, were thought to lend his site a little more protection.[13] Other Chinese internet companies like Tencent and Sohu subsequently launched their own versions, Tencent Weibo and Sohu Weibo, but while they have achieved limited success, Weibo remains shorthand for Sina Weibo, the site with the most users and highest traffic.

By the end of February 2011, Sina announced that its Weibo service already had more than 100 million users.[14] The company reported hitting 200 million registered users by August 2011, a number which had jumped to 309 million by the end of 2012 – approximately the population of the United States – and more than 600 million by late 2013.[15] It had become a crucial space for media and entertainment companies, as more and more Chinese internet users exploited the web to gather information.

One of the most interesting things about Weibo in mid-2011 – around the time of the Wenzhou train crash – was the inefficiency of its censorship. Like all social-media sites operating in the People's Republic, Weibo answered to government censorship authorities and agreed to censor sensitive content. Sina employs an army of censors, known colloquially as "little secretaries," who are charged with keeping such content at bay. Government departments periodically send updated lists of words and topics to the company, which passes the orders on to the little secretaries, who then delete posts, suspend or delete accounts, and disable searches for certain terms. But the lag between receiving an order and enforcing it seemed long enough that most interesting news was allowed to spread for at least a little while before it was deleted. In the site's earlier days, users could often see sensitive topics trend – and subsequently climb the charts on subpages that ranked keywords and hashtags by popularity in real time – before they were eventually deleted.

In the aftermath of the Wenzhou crash, authorities realized the potential for danger was higher than they'd thought, and took steps to keep activity on the site from boiling over. Just months after the two trains collided, authorities announced they would require all Weibo users to register with their real names. Perhaps awakened to the power that anonymous Weibo users had to question official reports without legal repercussions, the government saw safety in ensuring there could be consequences. On December 16, 2011, China's official news agency Xinhua reported that Beijing's city government had passed a real-name registration measure, to be implemented within three months.[16] Almost as an afterthought, Xinhua noted that the regulations also banned the posting of "illegal content," such as "information that leaks state secrets, damages national security and interests, and instigates ethnic resentment, discrimination or illegal rallies that disrupt social order."

Tied to their real identities, Weibo users would have more to fear when voicing an outspoken opinion. This push for real-name registration on Weibo was a repetition of previous pushes on other platforms, like blogs and forums, and the beginning of a larger movement to bring online spaces under the same restrictions as physical public spaces. But Sina and other sites were reluctant to enforce the policy, and many users found that their anonymous accounts remained useable even after the deadline for implementation had passed.

Money may have been the reason Sina was not so quick to the draw. Commercial forces driving Sina Weibo's success worked against censorship: Internet companies like Sina and Tencent were slow and uneven in their enforcement of the real-name registration system, perhaps in part because they feared losing users to their competitors: "Because domestic Chinese service providers know that the decision to weed out anonymous accounts could negatively affect content and drive away users," David Caragliano wrote on *Tea Leaf Nation*, "nobody wants to be the first to enforce the policy. Incentives lead to a kind of 'prisoner's dilemma' characterized by foot-dragging."[17]

Sina Weibo was right to be afraid. The implementation of such restrictions in the past had led to mass exoduses from other sites and lower rates of activity. Some users of a popular Tsinghua University bulletin board system (BBS) forum even held a memorial ceremony when the policy was implemented for their site, claiming that the rules spelled an end to its free-spirited culture.[18]

The real-name registration push following the Wenzhou crash marked the beginning of a larger conversation about censorship on the site. Some saw the policy as a curtailing of Weibo's power; others pointed out that it was an empty threat.[19] But whether or not real-name registration had sentenced Weibo to eventual irrelevance, as it had done to other platforms in the past, the specter of increasing censorship had already begun to loom.

A censored internet: good or bad?

Debate about censorship is nothing new, but it intensified around Weibo because the small victories that users had been able to achieve via the site inspired hope for greater freedom of speech. Given the complexity of censorship in China and the difficulty of ascertaining just how much activism has been allowed on Weibo, it's no surprise that opinion is divided as to whether Weibo has benefited or harmed China's burgeoning civil society.

Tech evangelists saw Weibo as a force for positive change, while skeptics pointed out that it could just as easily be used to manipulate and control public debate. Some have argued that Weibo was a force for political reform, a place where people could speak out and be heard. Others saw it as merely a "safety valve" that authorities tolerated because it allowed disgruntled Chinese to let off steam they might otherwise use to push for change, or diverted their attention from political matters.

Believers in the power of Weibo to change China have plenty of examples to cite: The platform has been used to track down and expose corrupt officials for years. Among the many fallen mighty, some have been caught wearing extravagantly expensive watches in official pictures, or smoking pricey cigarettes that an honest official could never afford. Once those pictures went viral, higher-level government bodies felt pressured to respond and launch investigations, many of which have resulted in officials losing their jobs and even going to jail.

Furthermore, outcry on Weibo has forced policy change. In one instance, in February 2013, Professor Yu Jianrong, the head of the Rural Development Institute of the Chinese Academy of Social Sciences, asked Weibo users to send him photos of luxury cars with license plates indicating that the drivers belonged to the military. Weibo users had long complained that members of the military were driving luxury cars obtained through abuse of privilege, disobeying traffic laws, and acting like they owned the roads. After Yu collected and shared thousands of these images, including some of expensive cars like Porches and Bentleys, China's Central Military Commission announced it was issuing a ban on most luxury vehicles.[20]

On the other hand, some scholars have argued against cherry-picking stories like these, warning that it paints an overly rosy picture of the net as it functions in Chinese society. Rebecca MacKinnon likened China's censored internet to a gilded cage in her book *Consent of the Networked: The Worldwide Struggle for Internet Freedom*. She concluded that unless there is a change in the status quo, there might be reason to believe that "the internet's pervasive use in China will actually help *prolong* the Communist Party's rule of China rather than hasten its demise."[21]

Many observers agree with her, shining a spotlight on the limits of successes like the campaign against military luxury vehicles. Gady Epstein also evoked the cage metaphor in *The Economist*, arguing that Weibo's successes mostly took place at the lowest levels, allowing higher authorities to solidify control:

Yet for the party as a whole the internet holds much less terror than it does for local officials. The online mob can gorge itself on corrupt low-level officials because the party leaders allow it. It can make fun of censorship, ridicule party propaganda and mock the creator of the Great Firewall. It can lampoon a system that deletes accounts and allows them to pop up again under a new name, only for the new accounts to be deleted in turn. It can rattle the bars of a cage all it likes. As long as the dissent remains online and unorganised, the minders do not seem to care.[22]

Jon Sullivan, a professor of contemporary Chinese studies at the University of Nottingham, has voiced a similar prediction: "Netizens will likely continue to use Weibo to publicize localized incidences of low level malfeasance, and the central government may allow them to proceed and may sometimes intervene," he wrote in a paper for *New Media & Society*:

> But wherever a Weibo event holds potential to grow beyond the parameters of localized discontent, the state will implement its censorship and propaganda regime, reinforced by control of technological infrastructure, legal and political leverage over internet companies and by marshalling physical world public security apparatus.[23]

In short, the central government benefits by appearing to be responsive to public opinion. This form of adaptive authoritarianism is adaptive but ultimately still authoritarian.

Even when Weibo was at its most vibrant – in 2010 and 2011, and to a lesser extent in 2012 and 2013 – some argued that it was little more than another tool by which the government could control public sentiment. Online speech could be monitored just like offline speech – if not more effectively – critics warned, and the government could use the tools developed by internet users against them. Weibo's push toward real-name registration, which would require users to provide identifying information when registering an account, seemed to bolster their points.

These skeptical arguments hold water. There is little more dangerous than blind optimism about a relatively new development, and, as it is written in the *Tao Te Ching*: "There is no greater misfortune than underestimating one's opponent." But there is more to Weibo than whether it helps achieve or undermine a particular political aim. A better understanding of how ordinary Chinese have reacted to censorship – and circumvented it – reveals not only creative forms of protest, but also underlying shifts in culture, philosophy, and society.

Censorship is no longer merely a way Chinese authorities can control information – despite their best efforts, it has become a shared experience that creates social bonds. Weibo users sympathize with one another over deleted posts and stymied discussions, calling out the censors and further raising awareness of the activity. Censors continue to delete posts that have collective-action potential as they understand it – a call to meet at a particular place and time, or information about a sensitive incident that could inspire offline action – but this focus leaves out smaller-scale, subtle connections that strengthen over time.

Further complicating matters for those who would "cleanse" China's web, the country's social surfers have become adept at outwitting censors, both man and machine, by using close homophones, code words, and oblique phrasing in their online speech. Censorship in China is no more innovative than censorship circumvention, especially on Weibo, where users crowdsource their strategies in real time.

While the punishment and intimidation of users who write on sensitive issues deter some, they also push others to take a more active role in combating censorship. Instead of accessing the internet directly, they use virtual private network (VPN) software to bypass China's censorship apparatus.

While few take the time to do so, they often share the information they obtain with others, spreading it within the borders of China's internet.

Increased awareness of censorship among ordinary people has also contributed to its ineffectiveness, and in some cases caused it to backfire. Searches on Baidu, China's largest search engine, or Sina Weibo, its largest microblogging platform, are censored as well: "Sensitive" terms often yield the following result: "In accordance with relevant laws, regulations and policies, search results for [term] cannot be displayed." Prior to the advent of the internet, a much smaller group of people came into contact with professional censors: mainly publishers, writers, journalists, and other professionals. Now, almost every internet user has experienced censorship first-hand.

Many users have also seen their posts deleted or accounts suspended. In a "randomized experimental study of censorship in China," conducted by Gary King, Jennifer Pan, and Margaret Roberts, the researchers employed Chinese web users to post a variety of content on 100 social-media sites, including most of China's most popular blogging platforms. They found that two out of five posts were put under "review" before publication – that is, flagged via automated censorship software for review by a human censor. Of those, almost two-thirds never ultimately appeared online. By those numbers, about one-fourth of all submissions were blocked by human censors.[24] This personal experience creates an awareness of censorship in other aspects of Chinese society.

Government and private enterprise work hard – and often effectively – to curtail what they perceive to be undesired consequences of online connection. But while censorship is superficially effective, it's a short-term solution that does not address long-term consequences. The structure of China's social web is inherently more collective than the fragmented space for offline debate. Weibo users feel more invested in national conversations and know that they have something in common with each other, regardless of their location within China or their circumstances.

On Weibo, more so than on any previous platform, the punishment of individual users is more public than ever before. And while cracking down on envelope-pushers discourages some, it also sets a fire under others, who become more motivated to fight back against these injustices. The scale and scope of censorship is daunting, but it also serves as a bright, attractive target for the many users who want something better for their country.

"Fuck your mother" and the anti-censorship movement

This is the unintended consequence of China's massive censorship campaign: As the country's internet censorship has moved out into the open, it has encountered increasing pushback from Chinese users. And in China, the movement against internet censorship has a mascot as cute as any you might find in children's cartoons. The "grass-mud horse," or *caonima* in Chinese, resembles a fluffy alpaca, but its peculiar name is a homophone for the slightly less cute phrase "Fuck your mother."

Initially, web users lashing out at each other wrote out the homophone to bypass automated censorship mechanisms that blocked foul language. Over time, however, the grass-mud horse came to symbolize anger with the censorship itself, and the "mother" referred to the Party (which often describes itself as the mother of the people).[25]

Caonima is ubiquitous on Weibo, where censorship is apparent to virtually all users. Even those who refrain from posting anything subversive have seen notices like: "Sorry, the original text has been deleted." So, to avoid automated censorship of curse words, Chinese users exclaim "Grass-mud horse!"

Weibo's in-house censorship team might be capable of ridding their site of the grass-mud horse, but it would take substantial effort, and users would likely latch on to another homophone. Already stretched thin scrubbing out controversial news stories, calls for protests, and pornographic images, Weibo censors know they have to choose their battles – and in this case, they have let *caonima* win.

But if you give a mouse a cookie, he's going to want some milk to go with it. Along with the grass-mud horse, Chinese netizens (*wangmin*, a portmanteau of "net" and "citizen" that is widely used in China) reference a number of fictional creatures to poke fun at censorship. The river crab, for instance, is pronounced *hexie*, a homophone for "harmonization" – a euphemism for censorship. The proliferation of seemingly silly wordplay represents a new normal, one in which subversive attitudes toward censorship and established ideologies are gaining ground.

This wordplay is a common form of Chinese humor: the act of pushing the envelope, saying just as much as one can without censure. In Chinese this is known as "serving up a border ball," one that in tennis or ping-pong might brush the line but ultimately stays within bounds. This verbal skill – implying criticism while allowing for plausible deniability – requires a firm grasp of the political landscape. Some of the funniest jokes are incredibly oblique: They depend on the audience having a wealth of knowledge about Chinese censorship. These jokes both entertain and reinforce the importance of that knowledge. Those who understand the jokes feel a connection with the people who tell them, and those who don't understand the jokes are motivated to learn the lay of the land.

Of course, the advanced technological side of China's censorship means that much of the more straightforward keyword blocking and search disabling may be automated. But Chinese internet users are adept at finding ways around these mechanisms. Some words, in the vein of *caonima*, were coined to bypass such censorship and are inherently subversive. For example, Chinese netizens use the abbreviation "ZF" for *zhengfu*, which means government, or call China *Tianchao*, the "Celestial Empire." Eventually, censorship programs are updated to track these variations, but they remain in use out of habit. The use of "ZF" instead of *zhengfu* indicates a certain degree of defiance. In China, such wordplay can also be a statement of attitude toward the government, or at least toward censorship.

Because of the extent of internet censorship in China, the space has seen an explosion of new words and new ways of using words. Known as internet language, the new linguistic patterns dwarf the "netspeak" of the English-speaking world in breadth and depth. Even Weibo users who do not comment on politics at all have picked up some of the habits of more political users by association.

It can be a bit extreme. For a period of several years, for example, many internet users even used homophones for words like "what" and "how." The Ministry of Education and older generations have decried the practice, but as always, the youth have persisted. In a sense, automation of censorship has trained Chinese internet users to redraw battle lines and reframe debates in real time. Shifting discourse and building momentum, these netizens force Chinese authorities to answer them on their terms.

It's no surprise, with this outpouring of creativity, that there are new nicknames for virtually everything. CCTV, for example, stands for China Central Television, but netizens often call it CCAV (China Central Adult Video) to imply that the news it produces – often regulated and restricted by censorship and propaganda authorities – is just as fake as porn. *Global Times*, a Communist Party mouthpiece famous for its hard-line stances and doublethink, earned the nickname *Global Turd*. In a similar vein, internet users will occasionally talk about the state-run *People's Daily* in equally disparaging terms – it doesn't hurt that the characters for "newspaper press," *ri bao she*, sound remarkably similar to "fuck explosive ejaculation." Chinese, with its more limited number of syllables, is absolutely full of homophones. On top of that, any given syllable could have a variety of meanings. Depending on the tone, "*ma*" can mean "mother," "marijuana," "horse," or "scold." This kind of wordplay is as easy in Chinese as rhyming is in Spanish.

Some feel that this wordplay is not an entirely positive development: "Chinese are a smart people, so they invented the river crab, sausage, Sparta, the pearl," wrote blogger Li Chengpeng, referencing some of the subversive neologisms that have proliferated in the internet age. "I also often use these remarks or jokes, but from a certain point of view, it seems that it isn't the development of new words, but the withering of speech."[26] The fear is that China's internet users, so used to speaking sideways, might forget how to say things straight out.

Yet humor, though base at times, can still influence public opinion. Subversive humor plants and waters seeds of skepticism in Chinese society, creating a new kind of culture and a new attitude toward the government. The aforementioned wordplay is just one subcategory of the subversive humor that thrives on the Chinese web, alongside parody videos, memes, cultural references, and much more. China's internet-censorship program, which targets collective action rather than criticism, can prevent protests but it cannot prevent more underlying shifts in the attitudes of ordinary Chinese toward their country and government, shifts that short-term publicity campaigns and financial investments cannot control effectively.

The digital is political

Up until this point, this book has talked about China's online sphere largely in terms of battle lines in the censorship struggle, and the linguistic landmines and virtual battle cries of those on both sides. This is all necessary information, but it is incomplete. What follows is equally true, but perhaps more important, because it fleshes out the nuances of China's online sphere, which often defies attempts by both the media and the government to simplify it.

Perhaps the most important aspect of the anti-censorship movement in China is that it is not a monolithic opposition. In fact, it is not a single movement, but many movements (and communities, and identities) that act in concert and opposition, that form and re-form, that evolve and adapt, that present a thousand different ideas of what is important and how to get things done. China's new internet cultures subvert the very idea that users must be this or that, patriots or critics, activists or apathetic. The next part of this chapter is an overview of some of these communities, their origins and their positions in China's online public square.

Mapping these communities brings into sharper focus how China's program of censorship has changed Chinese society and how, in many ways, the government is shooting itself in the foot by repressing so many voices of opposition.

To the left and right

To understand politics in China, it is important to know, first of all, that there is only one political party with any power: the Chinese Communist Party, or CCP. In fact, the CCP is so dominant that it goes by the shorthand "the Party." Simply put, the Party controls China's government at virtually every level. Discussion of China's politics often centers on forces working for and against the Party, protesters giving it their all against entrenched officials in good old David vs. Goliath fashion.

However, China's political landscape is a lot more complicated than the Party vs. Everybody Else. There is a spectrum of political beliefs that runs through Party and society alike, from the left – socialists who oppose capitalism, support collectivism, and decry interference from Western imperialism – to the right – those who call for a free-market economy, democracy, and human rights, as well as from apathy to activism, and everywhere in between. As Jeffrey Wasserstrom wrote in his book *China in the 21st Century*, one of the largest misconceptions about China is that it is a country of "only 'loyalists' and 'dissidents.'"[27]

Online, Weibo users come together in groups that do not exist neatly on a linear spectrum. Instead of simply declaring that they are pro- or anti-CCP, they have created "parties" of their own, bringing together people with similar political leanings and beliefs. These tongue-in-cheek self-identifications are humorous enough to defy a crackdown (China strictly controls the formation of political organizations), but meaningful enough to allow community bonding and action. And, importantly, such self-identifications subvert the CCP's assertion that loyalty to the Party is what makes one politically right or wrong.

One prime example of such a newly created "party" is the "Lead-the-way Party." Economically and politically liberal, these self-professed party members are known for criticizing corruption in China's government. This loosely connected community of like-minded individuals has its roots in online discussion of politics. According to the Chinese online encyclopedia *Baidu Baike*:

> [The term is] generally thought to have originated from the sarcastic remark, "If foreigners invade, I'll help the foreigners by leading the way." A typical case occurred in 2010 when the US and South Korea conducted multiple military exercises in the Yellow Sea. When a US aircraft carrier was going to enter the Yellow Sea, some people online said that if the US military invaded China, they would "lead the way." This self-identification, like "pi min" [slang roughly meaning "shitizen," or "nobody"], is self-mocking, and is mostly invoked to let off steam; it has also been used by some "patriotic" netizens as a stand-in for *hanjian* [meaning traitor] to mock those who oppose the current state of government and society, and who admire the people of Western countries.[28]

"Lead-the-way Party" is both a derogatory term and a badge of pride, depending on who's talking. People who profess to be members of the party have been subject to mockery and criticism online for lacking patriotism. Lead-the-way Party members often respond by saying that loving the country is not the same as loving the CCP. Furthermore, calling oneself a member of the Lead-the-way Party is not tantamount to supporting the overthrow of China's government in order to usher in another era of colonialism. The term is usually employed rhetorically, like threatening to move to another country if one's chosen political candidate doesn't win. What unites the members of the Lead-the-way Party is their unfavorable comparison of China's government to those of other countries. They criticize China's vast bureaucracy for rampant corruption and the CCP's focus on its image rather than its real problems.

On the other end of the spectrum from the Lead-the-way Party members are the so-called "angry youth," or *fenqing*. *Fenqing* are most often internet users in their twenties or thirties, usually students at university, with strong nationalist sentiment. Angry youth tend to be nostalgic for Mao Zedong, and often critical of foreign countries. They hate Japan, feel strongly about issues like Taiwan and Tibet, and use words like "Lead-the-way Party" and "traitor" to describe those they feel lack the appropriate amount of patriotism. Like "Lead-the-way Party," "angry youth" can be an insult or a compliment – depending on who's saying it. There even exists an exact homophone of the phrase *fenqing*, written with a different character, that literally translates as "shitty youth."

China's young leftists once had a home of their own on the Chinese internet, a website called Utopia that got more than 500,000 hits a day.[29] Utopia's members praised Maoist ideology and decried the growing income inequality brought about as China became a market economy. While US talking heads and political pundits often warn of the threat from "Communist China," the country's own leftists complain that China is no longer communist enough, having dismantled social safety nets and privatized much of its business. The website frequently criticized "rightists" for their love of Western ideas and criticism of China, publishing a list of "Western slaves" that should be "buried alive."[30] The list included noted liberal economist Mao Yushi, actor Jet Li, artist and activist Ai Weiwei, rights campaigner Xu Zhiyong, and dozens of others.[31]

It would be tempting to assume that members of the Lead-the-way Party and so-called "angry youth" belonged respectively to the anti- and pro-government camps on which narratives of China's internet rely. But in spite of their mutual animosity, China's leftist and rightist internet communities have more in common than might be apparent at first glance: Neither defines itself solely in relation to the CCP, and both have a bone to pick with the way China is currently run. "Angry youth" often lament that market reforms have exacerbated economic inequality, while Lead-the-way Party members believe market reforms without political reforms have led to similar inequality by fostering an oligarchic, authoritarian government. And especially when China's territorial disputes or ethnic tensions are concerned, these groups may even agree with each other.

In addition, no one ideological camp is safe from censorship and suppression. Though China's online left is quite nationalistic, even they have been kicked in the teeth by the government. The leftists active on Utopia were loyal to a set of ideals, not a political party, and were willing to criticize officials if they failed to live up to the community's expectations.

Eventually, Chinese authorities came down hard on Utopia for their support of a man China's top leaders viewed as a threat – Bo Xilai. By 2012, Utopia had gone all-in supporting Bo, a powerful Party official who was leading a leftist revival in central China and campaigning for a position in China's central leadership. When Bo fell in a political purge, authorities shut down Utopia, along with two other popular leftist websites.[32] The message was clear: Neither leftist angry youth nor rightist members of the Lead-the-way Party can rely on government protection.

This shared vulnerability hasn't fostered much mutual understanding. Angry youth accuse their ideological enemies of working for Western imperialists to undermine China's stability. Rightists fire back by saying that their nationalist counterparts belong to the "50-cent Party," or *Wumao Dang*, a derogatory term for internet commentators who secretly receive 50 Chinese cents per pro-government post. (The existence of these paid pro-government commentators is widely documented, and the CCP has always been quite open about the need for positive propaganda, which in Chinese has a more neutral connotation.)

The 50-cent Party complicates China's online landscape, because its existence throws shadows of suspicion and doubt onto all facets of online debate. The knowledge that some pro-government posts are insincere undermines the credibility of all pro-government rhetoric. Even worse, the acceptance of this practice leads many to question any and all online debate – after all, if the government can hire people to praise it online, so could anyone else.

A better understanding of how 50-centers operate makes it clear just how disruptive such propaganda can be. In early 2011, artist and activist Ai Weiwei offered an iPad to any member of the 50-cent Party willing to answer questions about his job, and one took him up on the offer.[33] Ai published the transcript of the interview, in which the unnamed commenter described his work as "easy" and a good way to make a little money on the side. When asked about the specific process, he elaborated:

Usually after an event has happened, or even before the news has come out, we'll receive an email telling us what the event is, then instructions on which direction to guide the netizens' thoughts, to blur their focus, or to fan their enthusiasm for certain ideas. After we've found the relevant articles or news on a website, according to the overall direction given by our superiors we start to write articles, post or reply to comments [...] In a forum, there are three roles for you to play: the leader, the follower, the onlooker or unsuspecting member of the public. The leader is the relatively authoritative speaker, who usually appears after a controversy and speaks with powerful evidence. The public usually finds such users very convincing. There are two opposing groups of followers. The role they play is to continuously debate, argue, or even swear on the forum. This will attract attention from observers. At the end of the argument, the leader appears, brings out some powerful evidence, makes public opinion align with him and the objective is achieved. The third type is the onlookers, the netizens. They are our true target "clients." We influence the third group mainly through role-playing between the other two kinds of identity. You could say we're like directors, influencing the audience through our own

writing, directing and acting. Sometimes I feel like I
have a split personality.

The interviewed commenter claimed that he could tell that
10 to 20 percent of all comments on online forums were
made by 50-centers. But he maintained that his job was "like
any other job. It's not as dark as you think."[34] China's giant
censorship and "public-opinion control" apparatus includes
many people like this: low-level, low-responsibility contributors who cannot bear the blame for the system itself. At the
highest levels, propaganda officials may be motivated by a
genuine belief that the public must be guided for their own
good. In addition to having a vested interest in preventing
"chaos," propaganda officials are accountable to each other
and their own leaders – and are themselves products of previous generations' propaganda efforts. There are culpable
individuals, and wrong policies, but no one person shoulders
the blame for strangling China's freedom of speech. Even
on the lowest levels, in online spats among paid commentators and would-be social critics, it would be wrong to say
that 50-centers are "The Enemy." They are merely another
element of the internet ecosystem, albeit not a very popular
or helpful one.

This ecosystem, limited as it is, has fostered any number
of identities like the Lead-the-way Party. Such semi-serious
self-affiliations slip under the radar of government interference. Their informality is also the source of their power:
Under the right circumstances, these pre-existing "parties"
can unite groups of like-minded people; when such conditions do not exist, the ties are invisible. The fluidity of these
identifications also defies the suppression of "political" individuals, because it reveals all individuals to be political to a

degree. Because Weibo's format emphasizes content while downplaying its source, it supports this fluidity in a way that previous formats have not.

Refusing to accept censorship: the Reincarnation Party

Beyond the left and right, there is another class of Weibo users who come back from the dead – or at least from account deletion. These netizens belong to the "Reincarnation Party," or *Zhuanshi Dang*. The term describes users who have registered new accounts after their previous handles have been shut down by Weibo censors. Users often register new account handles that reflect the number of times they've been reincarnated: for example, "WangPingLife3" would indicate that a user had reregistered after account deletion twice. Members of this party perceive reincarnation as a badge of honor, claiming that "to reincarnate is glorious."

The Reincarnation Party, unique to Weibo due to the prevalence of censorship, is an instance in which suppression as a shared experience has helped the suppressed bond and fight back. The persistence of reincarnated netizens reflects a commitment to fighting censorship. Their return to the site is a refusal to cede online space for debate to those who would silence them.

The Reincarnated often face real repercussions. Take Wu Yangwei for example. Wu, who uses the pen name Ye Du and serves as vice president of the Independent Chinese PEN Center, had previously been detained due to critical articles he had published online and interviews he had accepted from foreign media.[35] But even after experiencing these real-world consequences of his online speech, he continued to reincarnate on Weibo: "Every single reincarnation spreads freedom, dignity, and knowledge of right and wrong a little further," he wrote on the site. "Each one shows just a bit more the truth behind the 'moral superiority' of officials. That is how freedom comes into being: bit by bit."[36]

Another way Weibo users get around account deletion and suspension is by creating extra accounts – called "little handles," or "vests," these accounts can be maintained "just in case," and users often tell their friends to follow the little handles as well as their main accounts so that they won't lose touch in instances of account deletion.

All of these measures seem simple enough to see through – if Weibo's censorship team wanted to do so, couldn't they simply delete the "little handles" and the accounts of reincarnated users? It's true that Weibo censors can continue to delete accounts and block searches for and the publishing of certain content. But, so far, censors seem to be busy fighting other battles, and only seriously target a handful of reincarnated netizens, like Ai Weiwei.

Still, China's government does interfere in Weibo when issues are particularly sensitive, or when ordinary individuals push the envelope in a way that it deems unacceptable. These users then belong to another party: the "Tea-drinking Party" or *Hecha Dang*. Unlike the hyper-conservative US Tea Party, China's Tea-drinking Party members are so named because they have been invited to "drink tea" with the police or government officials, in meetings where they are asked about their political activities and warned not to make any more trouble.

Some Weibo users see being "forced to drink tea" as a badge of honor, just like reincarnation. Among some politically minded Chinese, though, drinking tea with officials is a regular occurrence, a source of frustration, even fodder for jokes. In addition to humor, there is also fear: Police have threatened to charge some users with "creating public disorder" or "spreading rumors" unless they give up their sources of information. In one more high-profile case, a Taiwanese actress named Annie Yi Nengjing lost a lucrative television contract after she refused to withdraw support for journalists in mainland China protesting censorship.[37]

Crowdsourcing activism: the Food-delivery Party

All of this is well and good, but what impact can the formation of online communities have on the real world? The answer is, a very real one. In 2011, like-minded Chinese netizens formed the Food-delivery Party, or *Songfan Dang*, to help Chinese activists detained, arrested, or jailed by authorities for their protests, as well as their families. The Food-delivery Party is a coordinated effort to provide them with money and other kinds of assistance through a number of online platforms and social-media campaigns.

Xu Zhirong, who goes by the nickname Rou Tangsen online, began the Food-delivery Party in 2011, when he contacted people he knew on Weibo to donate money for Ran Yunfei, a pro-democracy activist jailed for his participation in protests earlier that year. After successfully raising those funds, he asked his friends to help Tang Jitian, another rights activist. Heartened by the success of these campaigns, he took his pleas from direct messaging to public forums.

Members of the Food-delivery Party shared information about the group and its activities through Weibo. They circulated long essays and changed their avatars to the party's symbol: a man in a long robe delivering food. Though censorship hampered them somewhat, party members were able to raise some awareness of their cause through Weibo.

Amidst such positive feedback on Weibo, Rou took these campaigns to the next level by setting up an open platform on Taobao, China's eBay. As part of the campaigns, other Taobao stores could display a "Food-delivery Party" logo if they pledged to donate 5 to 8 percent of their profits to the cause. In just the first month that his online "store" (known as "Roupu") was open, he raised tens of thousands of dollars.[38]

What exactly was being sold to make money? The Taobao shop had normal items like clothing and purses, but also auctioned off essays and signed books, as well as face-to-face meetings with famous scholars. When raising money for Wang Dengchao, a policeman jailed for 14 years after he organized an event to honor a historical figure, Rou sold an essay that contained only two words: "Thank you."[39] Proceeds from the sale of that article alone totaled almost $20,000 in just 66 hours.

The platform and its operations were designed to be user-controlled. Anyone who donated became a committee member, and was occasionally selected to perform duties on the site. Though the platform was shut down in October 2013, the model and its success have inspired a number of similar platforms and operations. The Food-delivery Party is one of the best examples of an internet-native identity in China bridging the gap between virtual criticism and real action.

Same-city dinners

Perhaps one of the most important communities formed by the backlash against censorship and repression does not call itself a party. In fact, it does its best not to call itself anything at all, eschewing membership rosters, centralized leadership, and most other formalities. But it has led to offline meetings in more than 30 cities across China, which take place despite authorities' threats and surveillance.

These offline meetings are called "same-city dinners," or "citizen banquets" – localized gatherings of individuals to talk about politics, social issues, or anything else related to citizens' rights over dinner. The phrase "same-city dinner" seemed innocuous enough, but another word for the meeting, "food-drunk activity," a homophone for "criminal activity" in Chinese, is slightly more subversive. It refers to the fact that the same-city gatherings are just this side of legal. Chinese law forbids citizens from forming organizations without government approval, but these gatherings are informal enough not to break the law. Police have broken up some gatherings and left others alone; the gray area in which they take place is safer, at least, than a more codified system. Yet having a set date – the last Saturday of each month – gives the practice enough momentum to sustain itself.

There is conversation at these dinners, but also coordination. Participants may discuss points of concern and decide on plans of action over food and drink, and then separately carry out their activities online. They may decide to initiate an information campaign, call for the release of a prisoner of conscience via social media, or carry out a more involved plan of action.

The way these gatherings are connected is fluid enough that a single blow will not suffice to end the practice outright. Even when individuals are detained or particular dinner gatherings are broken up by the police, the activity itself keeps going. This decentralization of power, which in some ways does present an obstacle to organization, has made the movement far less vulnerable to intimidation tactics. If one gathering or person is targeted, they can also count on others throughout the country to draw attention to it.[40]

In the face of continuous assaults by censors, Chinese web users have continued to speak out against misinformation and support each other through times of hardship, often at great personal risk. Their actions have inspired others to stand up for their rights as well, growing social networks both off- and online.

In effect, the collective experience of censorship has brought online communities close together. Instead of stifling freedom of speech, it has only temporarily hampered it – and simultaneously fueled the fight for it. Though censorship has successfully slowed the spread of information and helped authorities put down protests, it is a losing move in the long run.

three

TECTONIC SHIFTS: COUNTERCULTURE ONLINE

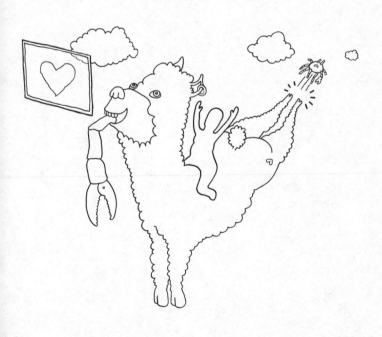

Often changes seem to happen in the blink of an eye: Two trains collide, or the earth begins to move. In such moments, things we never thought could happen show us how little we know about predicting the future. This is especially true of China, which continues to surprise even career analysts despite decades of collective induction and divination. The unpredictability of it all fuels a feverish kind of following. Any sudden movement in China seems to cause waves of anxiety to ripple through those who spend their days waiting for the country to either implode or invade.

Yet while the sudden and unexpected dominate our headlines and bookshelves, slow-moving shifts tend to get less press. Everything important about China as a country and society has been changing while most of us have been reading the news of the day. And though we periodically look to the past to evaluate China's development in economics and human rights, we spend far less time looking at changes in attitudes, opinions, ways of life, and philosophies. Softer and far harder to quantify, these transformations at the grass-roots level will shape the future of China and the world just as surely as the country's monetary policy or diplomacy will.

Though these changes have been happening for quite some time, the internet and Weibo in particular have accelerated them. They have empowered groups that would challenge mainstream opinion and accelerated tipping points in shifts of opinion and attitude. Weibo has broken down the barriers that made people think they were alone. It has helped people connect the dots, forming a bigger picture of systemic problems from individual grievances. And most importantly, Weibo has made it possible for Chinese to organize grass-roots resistance to those problems. Accelerated, these once-imperceptible shifts have become visible to the naked eye.

Across China, people have begun to change their minds on pretty fundamental questions, like: "What is success?" "Who deserves respect?" and "Is it wrong to be different?" From economics to politics, sexuality to sexism, public opinion is shifting in support of equality, tolerance, and justice. The following pages explore these changes, and how Weibo played a part in them.

Great expectations: who defines success?

One of the most significant transformations going on in China right now is a mass shifting of attitudes and values – specifically, among young Chinese in their twenties and thirties. In almost every country, young adults tend to be at the fore-front of calls for change, and China is no exception. China's youth today are redefining what it means to be successful, and in the process, challenging decades and even centuries of convention and tradition.

Complicating this is the fact that China's rapid transfor-mation since the early 1980s has created a generation gap of epic proportions. Younger generations take for granted the country's economic growth and the freedom to choose their own paths. They have been able to study abroad, get college educations, and start their own businesses. And just as importantly, they are the first generation in China to utilize the internet to its full potential.

Their elders, on the other hand, were born into poverty and raised in a highly regulated and repressed era. Today's grandparents and parents grew up during the Great Leap Forward and Cultural Revolution. Food was rationed and sometimes very scarce, jobs and homes assigned by work units, and individuals had very little latitude in terms of how they chose to live their lives. The collective good was valued above the individual, and many internalized the unspoken rules for survival: Obey orders, guard your tongue, and be grateful for what you have. These generations were already middle-aged by the time China began to open up and reform, in the late 1970s and early 1980s. While they have benefited from China's reforms, by and large they retain the values and mindsets developed in their younger days.

The urban youth of China's cities enjoy freedoms their parents and grandparents never did, but they also shoulder the sometimes unreasonable hopes – for financial success, happy marriages, and influence in the community – of their elders. Many of China's middle-aged saw their own hopes and dreams ground to dust in the country's collectivist machine, and they desperately want better for their children. When they look at Chinese society today, they see so many opportunities for success. Why then, they wonder, have their children not lived up to their expectations?

It's simply harder to see much of what's holding back China's youth today – unless you're looking for it. In the old days, someone's stamp in your permanent file could bar you from your dream job. Young Chinese today might still experience professional setbacks, but they are more insidious.

Perhaps the job they wanted went to the boss's cousin, or the son of someone with connections. Maybe the employer didn't find their headshot – a standard fixture in Chinese CVs – pretty enough. Despite the lifted restrictions on private enterprise, corruption, poverty, and politics still hold many back. These subtle restrictions are all too apparent to China's youth, who experience them daily, but it is less easy for their older family members to understand and sympathize.

To add frost on top of snow, as the Chinese saying goes, many younger people in China are only children, born after the country's government began to implement the one-child policy in 1979. The policy, which tried to curb China's population growth in order to ameliorate certain social, environmental, and economic problems, restricted most urban couples to a single child. In the past, Chinese families had multiple children, who shared the burdens of caring for their elderly parents and grandparents, but, as a result of the policy, many young adults in China are facing the daunting reality that they may be expected to care for six aging adults.

As only children, they cannot fail – their parents' and grandparents' futures likely depend on their economic success. They must pass the highly competitive *gaokao*, or college entrance examination, and attend a good school. They must then enter a tough job market – studies show that over recent years China's job market for recent graduates has gotten steadily worse – and find a good, stable job in an ever-changing economy that is finally showing signs of fatigue. Furthermore, being only children, younger Chinese feel obligated to marry and carry on the family line – not doing so is considered the worst failure in Confucian filial piety. Most of this pressure – to study, work, wed, and procreate – falls on them all at once, in their twenties and early thirties.

Birth of a counterculture

China's youth are expected to be healthy, wealthy, and socially successful, but as in any country, many are fat, poor, and awkward. With all of these pressures, it is no wonder that they have pushed back against outwardly imposed expectations. Embracing their less than perfect identities, many Chinese identify as or empathize with *diaosi* – a term coined online that roughly means "loser" – but with one key difference, as explained by the website Civil China:

> Although "diaosi" is often translated as "loser" in English, our analysis points to a distinction between a Chinese "diaosi" and a "loser": losers are responsible for their own lack of success, while diaosi are made by larger social conditions. No wonder then, that "loser" remains an indisputably negative term, personal in its injury, while "diaosi" is a true meme: dynamic, complex, and current, cultural rather than personal.[1]

Even the etymology of *diaosi* is coarse. The term, which literally means "dick hair," traces its origins to a back-and-forth flame war in an obscure online forum devoted to football.[2] Yet from such humble beginnings, it went on to become perhaps the most popular online slang of 2012. For a while, it was everywhere on the Chinese internet.

Surveys of young internet users also shed light on the *diaosi* demographics. Computer programmers and media professionals, who also tend to be younger, are the most likely to identify as *diaosi*, while government officials are the least.[3] The former group is more likely to see the system as an obstacle to success, while the latter hope to achieve success within the system. From these surveys, it's clear that many *diaosi* are tech-savvy and early adopters – trendsetters – while those who are least likely to call themselves "dick hair" are the most conservative and risk-averse segment of society.

Some prominent celebrities like director Feng Xiaogang have come out against the word, calling it an insult, but many ordinary Chinese have embraced it as a way of asserting that even a lowly life is legitimate.[4] Even those who would not identify as *diaosi* themselves enjoy rooting for the underdogs in online banter.

The internet has played a great role in making such countercultural trends more acceptable. And while web users tend to be younger than non-surfers in almost every corner of the world, this trend is especially pronounced in China. Over 80 percent of those who frequent social-media sites in China are less than 40 years old.[5] On Weibo alone, almost 90 percent of users are under 40, so it should come as no surprise that jokes, stories, and discussions about *diaosi* proliferate there.

Diaosi are up against terrible odds, and China's youth can identify with that. While most Chinese youth still aspire to success – they would rather be employed and lucky in love than poor and lonely – they wish that it was more acceptable to acknowledge the role economic and social pressures have played in marginalizing a large proportion of China's population.[6]

Where society has expected financial success, China's younger citizens have embraced less flashy identities – by discussing, debating, and claiming their identities as *diaosi*. Where social rules dictate respect for the wealthy and powerful, jokes about China's nouveau riche abound on Weibo. Weibo's ability to challenge traditional structures of prestige and power has made it particularly appealing to younger users and those with fewer advantages in traditional society. Many have enjoyed the way the site allows them relative freedom to explore alternative worldviews and criticize the mainstream.

For many young Chinese, career and financial troubles can also make it difficult to find love. In traditional Chinese culture, marrying and having children is highly valued, but, these days, money has further complicated romance: Many men feel pressured to own their own apartments before women will take them seriously. And it's a whopping three times as expensive for a Chinese person to buy a home in Beijing as it is for an American to buy one in New York, when average income and property prices are factored in.[7] A significant number of Chinese could save their whole lives and never be able to afford a run-down apartment in China's capital.

It's no walk in the park for women either. Leta Hong Fincher wrote in her book *Leftover Women* that women are putting their hard-earned cash toward ridiculously expensive mortgages as well – but often their names are not included in the deeds. Instead of helping daughters put down payments on property, she found, they offered their help to male relatives.[8] In short, at the intersection of money and love, very few people are getting fair deals – and some are getting worse deals than others.

Cash to burn

The problem is not just that some Chinese don't have enough money – it's also that some have more than they know what to do with. The very visible wealth disparity between China's outrageously well-off and the people who clean their toilets has made success seem that much further away for young people from lower- and middle-class backgrounds. In earlier days, having a regular job might be good enough, but since China has become more of a market economy, wealth – the more the better – is now prized.

It was not so long ago that "capitalist" was a dirty word in China. Certainly it was verboten during the early days of the People's Republic, where "capitalist roaders" and "capitalist running dogs" could face imprisonment or worse. But even in the 1990s, after China's economic reforms had already borne fruit, societal and political barriers remained for would-be entrepreneurs.[9] Regulations made it difficult to run large private companies despite ample economic incentives, leading many to wear "red hats" – running private companies while calling them "collective enterprises." These entrepreneurs sometimes still experienced a degree of scorn in society at large, and most were excluded from the CCP – at least on paper.

But in 2002, China's leaders came out in support of the country's businesspeople, declaring that the erstwhile capitalist roaders were performing honorable work for the country. In the years since, the Party has sought to bring the financially successful into the fold, often allowing them to sit as delegates in the National People's Congress. In part due to this strategy of co-opting entrepreneurs, the collective net worth of China's legislators is enormous. The richest 50 delegates in the National People's Congress control almost $100 billion, while the richest 50 US congresspeople are worth only $1.6 billion combined, as of 2013.[10]

Adding to this the conflation of economic development and the country's health, and it's no wonder that the early 2000s were a time of rampant conspicuous consumption in China. A class of nouveau riche found themselves suddenly bestowed with both money and social status, and they flaunted it. Ordinary Chinese, seeing the increasing interconnectedness of power and money, accepted the new rules and developed survival mechanisms even as many complained about the growing cancer of materialism.

Yet the mainstream idea that "to get rich is glorious" – a quote often attributed to Deng Xiaoping, but in fact of unknown origins – indirectly led to the stigmatization of China's poor, who still number in the hundreds of millions. For a decade or more, dissatisfaction grew as mainstream culture continued to validate the wealthy while social mobility declined and the wealth gap grew. A few more countercultural Chinese chose to "opt out" here or there, but their voices were isolated. When Chinese internet users began to rally behind the *diaosi* identity, they also formed a group that could stand apart from mainstream ideas of success and critique them.

With Weibo, it became clear that sympathy for the *diaosi* narrative was not a countercultural movement on the margins, but in fact a subculture strong enough to rival the mainstream. The shift in language used to talk about *diaosi*, the skyrocketing popularity of the term, and the number of "upvotes" related posts began to get all pointed to a central truth: Fewer and fewer Chinese were buying into the idea that theirs was a meritocratic society.

As Chinese have revised their views on society's "losers," their feelings toward traditional "winners" have changed as well. Just as *diaosi* developed as an identity supported by a philosophy, internet users shared their dissatisfaction with mainstream values and China's new materialism. They even began to mock the wealthy, in a reserved fashion, by calling them *tuhao*.

Tuhao, literally meaning "dirt splendor," went viral on Chinese social media in 2013. It referred to China's tacky but powerful nouveau riche, also known as "China's Beverly Hillbillies." The term is roughly interchangeable with "new money" except for a few unique connotations.[11] Despite coming into circulation fairly recently, the term *tuhao* has older origins. It was used in the 1950s, when land reform was being conducted, to refer to the landed gentry. During that time, the CCP organized poorer groups to struggle against the once wealthy, shouting slogans like "beat the *tuhao*, divide the field." But as with most old political terminology, *tuhao* fell out of use as the country moved out of its revolutionary phase.

In more recent decades, Chinese have begun to dust off old jargon like *tuhao* and use it ironically, a trend that has been particularly pronounced online. In the 1990s, the word "comrade" became slang for "homosexual." In the 1990s and 2000s, art galleries began to appropriate and remix the imagery of the Cultural Revolution, selling Communist kitsch, like T-shirts bearing Maoist slogans. In the past few years, words used in Imperial China have begun to circulate online once more.[12] The revived vocabulary speaks to the parallels between China's feudal past – where power and wealth were concentrated in the hands of the few – and contemporary China – where income inequality has grown once more under an authoritarian government.

Tuhao are thought powerful but oblivious, wealthy but without taste, and are a subject of collective mockery in a way that those referred to by earlier Chinese terms for new money, like *baofahu*, never were.

Weibo users made jokes about the term and began to use it as an adjective describing an awkwardly excessive use of wealth or status. Even Apple got dragged into the mix when they released the new iPhone 5s in "champagne gold" – or, as Weibo users dubbed it, "*tuhao* gold." The *People's Daily* building was also dubbed "*tuhao* gold," when it received a gold-colored facade.

How does Weibo factor into the rise of these new attitudes? Weibo allowed terms like *diaosi* and *tuhao* to go viral. Online, the gradually growing middle class of China – for whom good taste is at least a consolation prize for unattainable wealth – rallied suddenly to take this stance against conspicuous consumption, with usage of the term *tuhao* spiking sharply in early October of 2013.

The catalyst for the sudden chatter about *tuhao* was an article published in Chinese domestic media about a wedding in China's relatively poor Anhui province. The bride's mother gave her son-in-law a Bentley, and all of the wedding guests received gifts of cash as well. The diverse reactions to the article – which some say was a fictional account – reflected the complex feelings Chinese had about the position of *tuhao* in their society. There was jealousy as well as mockery, derision as well as acceptance.[13]

Amid this renewed referencing of income and power inequalities, disdain for the children of the wealthy – *fu'erdai*, or "rich second-generation," as they are known – has surged on Weibo, where the cash-strapped complain about their finances in the same online space that children of millionaires post pictures of their latest extravagant purchases. Images, which can go viral in a heartbeat, can be particularly incendiary. One woman found herself the target of online vitriol after she posted a picture of herself in a dress made of cash, claiming her "sugar daddy" had given it to her. Another uploaded a shot of a bouquet of cash she had received. A less creative Weibo user simply showed off stacks of China's red currency. The rich kids of the Middle Kingdom have found that they may easily become scapegoats or touchstones for the masses of less privileged netizens.[14] In part this reflects anger about a lack of social mobility in China, and in part it stems from anger about injustice, because the rich are assumed to be above the law.

The rise of *diaosi* and *tuhao* are just two of many linguistic trends that point to a greater change that is happening in China right now: an online, public re-examining of wealth and values. Thanks in part to Weibo, dissatisfaction with China's income gap reached a tipping point, and younger Chinese began to question the materialism that had run rampant for more than a decade. The result is a cultural consensus that money is useful, but it's not everything – that what's really important is to give it your best shot, even if you know you're going to lose.

Full frontal defiance: Weibo activism

While broad swaths of Chinese society have banded together on Weibo over income inequality, veteran activists have also drawn strength and momentum from the platform for their own causes. In particular, groups that have historically experienced discrimination, including feminists and LGBT-rights activists, have used China's new online spaces to advance their causes in ways that would have been impossible even ten years earlier.

These activists have benefited from Chinese social media in two main ways. Firstly, they have been able to network and support each other on Weibo and other platforms. In the past, online forums devoted to these causes have come under attack from hackers and others opposed to their efforts – such tactics were less effective against the more loose-knit communities that formed on Weibo. Secondly, as members of these communities are also integrated into other online networks, they are better able to make their voices heard outside activist communities.

Naked feminists, bared blades

China's feminists have seen how useful Weibo can be and have exploited it. Challenging conservative ideas about a woman's place in society, they have fought for gender equality in the law and against the victimization of women by those in power.

Activist Ye Haiyan is one such woman. In May of 2013, she heard of a terrible incident in which a school principal from China's Hainan Island and a government official were caught taking six primary-school girls to a hotel room, where they were drugged and raped.[15] Ye took to her Weibo account and posted a picture of herself holding up a sign that read: "Principal: get a room with me, leave the young schoolchildren alone!" The number she added at the bottom of the sign was that of a hotline for women's rights services.[16] Her act drew support; thousands of other Weibo users took their own pictures and posted them online.[17]

The viral protest raised awareness of growing dissatisfaction with widespread abuse of power. The case enraged many, as it belonged to a much larger trend of school employees and government officials using their power to harm minors: At least seven such cases had come to light in early 2013.[18] The fact that the case represented the intersection of several controversial issues also encouraged solidarity among different activist communities online.

This was not the first time that Ye had used social media to spread her message. She has more than 73,000 followers on Sina Weibo and more than 88,000 on Tencent Weibo.[19]

She's also an active user of Twitter, where she has more than 22,000 followers.[20] She posts almost daily on all three platforms, conversing with other activists about goals and updating followers on her activities. Like many, Ye found that social media offers an unparalleled platform for raising awareness, especially because she lacked the standing in traditional fields of power – being a self-taught, grass-roots activist with only a junior-high-school education – that might earn her a seat at the table.[21]

Ye did not become a social-media sensation overnight. In the beginning, she was just the manager of a karaoke club in central China. But after she witnessed a sex worker being beaten there – while police stood by and did nothing – she was forced to act. When she later divorced her husband and moved out with her daughter, she stayed with a number of sex workers who offered her their home. After hearing more of their stories, she started a website in 2005 so that they would have a place to express themselves without experiencing discrimination.[22]

For the better part of a decade, Ye helped sex workers and other women throughout China in quiet ways, giving them a space to talk to each other, listening to their stories, and working with them to solve their problems. As she became more well known, she picked bigger fights, demanding greater protection for women and an end to discrimination against sex workers.

In one of her more influential campaigns, Ye sought to draw support for sex workers by serving as one for two and a half days.[23] In early 2012, she volunteered to provide free sex services at a low-cost brothel and spoke with the migrant workers who frequented it. To raise awareness, she live-posted her experience on Weibo, sharing the stories of her encounters with four men. Social media was heavily divided, with some calling Ye brave and others saying she was immoral.[24] Her unconventional methods of lobbying for women, sex workers, and AIDS patients has drawn criticism from conservatives – embracing her somewhat controversial status, she calls herself "Hooligan Yan."

Through Weibo, Ye has worked with others pursuing the same goals, including Ai Xiaoming, a retired professor at Sun Yat-sen University in Guangzhou. Ai, another noted feminist, was the first woman to obtain a PhD in China when schools were reopened after the Cultural Revolution, and she was the first to bring *The Vagina Monologues* to a stage in China.[25] When Ye was detained for using a knife to defend herself against women who attacked her in her home, Ai posed topless, bearing a sign that said: "Get a room with me, and leave Ye Haiyan alone!"[26]

Like Ye, Ai also used her body in a very public way on social media, to protest for change while chipping away at the stigma surrounding women and sex in China. In an interview with internet portal NetEase, Ai explained why she felt the naked female body was powerful. "The female body is too often defined as an object of desire," she told her interviewer. "I wanted to express opposition [...] you took Ye Haiyan away in handcuffs, that's her human body. Well then, I'm going to show you my human body, to tell you, I'm not afraid, I can take you on."[27] Ai's and Ye's courage has inspired others to do the same. In fact, naked pictures have become a form of protest used by other critics in China to express dissent.

When Ye was evicted after the knife incident, Ai gave her and her daughter a place to stay.[28] Their bond is not merely one of shared interests but shared beliefs; their shared community online has created and strengthened their real-world connections and support systems. Like universities, social-media platforms have fostered communities of ideas in which like-minded people develop real relationships. But social media has allowed people from different provinces and even different countries to connect, and it allows greater freedom of expression than many universities in China.

Both Ye and Ai have shown that Weibo can help bring issues like sex workers' rights from their usual position at the margins of national debate to the forefront. In her activism before Weibo, Ye ran a website in a small corner of China's internet. Using social media, she's brought her causes into the center of the room.

Fighting back against abusers

Weibo was also an important battleground for the fight against domestic violence in 2011. That year, a woman named Kim Lee uploaded pictures of injuries received at the hands of her husband, a wealthy and famous businessman named Li Yang. She had come from the police station, where an officer reluctantly took down her report of the obvious violence she suffered, and turned to social media to make her case known. The graphic pictures she posted of her bleeding ear, swollen forehead, and bruised knees drew wide media coverage within China and forced Li to respond to the accusations in an interview with the *China Daily*. He admitted he "hit her sometimes," but emphasized that he never believed that Lee would go public with these accusations, "since it's not Chinese tradition to expose family conflicts to outsiders."[29]

Yet Kim Lee found support, rather than admonishment, online. In an interview with the *New York Times*, Lee said that she had received more than 1,000 messages of support from strangers since she made the abuse public over a year before on Weibo.[30] Many of her posts received even more comments, from users criticizing Li Yang and calling for a change in China's laws.

"I once wanted to endure, and tried to change, a man like Li Yang," commented one Weibo user, on one of Kim Lee's posts about the abuse. "In the end I discovered I was wrong. All of my work was in vain. Get a divorce. Split his assets. Live a happy life with your children."

"We cannot tolerate this kind of thing," wrote another. "Li Yang's craziness is a perversion, we can't let him do whatever he wants. Use legal means to stop him."

"Remember that we are all on your side!" a woman from Guangdong wrote. "And you'll know you have a circle of friends on the internet."[31]

Taking to social media was effective for Lee. The picture of her bleeding ear was reposted more than 24,000 times.[32] Her husband asked her by text message to take down her posts about the abuse, but she persisted. In February 2013, Kim Lee received one of the first restraining orders in China (the very first restraining order for a domestic-violence victim was issued only two years earlier, in 2011).[33] She had reached the end of her long battle to divorce her abusive husband, and was granted full custody as well as some financial compensation.

Kim Lee now has almost 70,000 followers on Weibo, far more than she had when she began to speak out about her experience of domestic violence. She continues to share articles about women's rights and domestic violence, as well as answer media queries. When she took Li to court, her supporters accompanied her and stood in protest outside, with their faces painted to resemble those of battered women.

Chinese activists have been working against domestic violence for years, but it has not been easy. The *Beijing Evening News* reported that while suits for divorce citing domestic violence had increased in the city (from 34 in 2011 to 114 in 2012, and then 104 in the first nine months of 2013 alone), only one out of every five suits was accepted. According to judicial interpretations, the harm done to the victim must meet a certain threshold before it is considered domestic violence, though the wording does not provide specific criteria.[34] In 2011, the All China Women's Federation found that 20 percent of all Chinese women experienced domestic violence, and remarked that corresponding legislation was insufficient.[35]

Kim Lee has become a symbol for those who want a tougher stance on domestic violence in China. Though some say that Lee, an American, does not represent Chinese women, she has set legal precedents in her divorce case, settled in Chinese courts, and she lives with her three children in China. And by making her case public, she helped fight taboos against exposing "dirty laundry."

China's favorite porn star

As Chinese society becomes more open about domestic violence, it is also becoming more open about sex. While conservatism continues to exert a powerful influence, many younger Chinese are using online hookup apps, having premarital sex, admitting they watch pornography, and not apologizing for it. And this massive movement toward greater sexual openness has its own fearless leader: Sola Aoi.

Who is Sola Aoi? She's a petite, 30-year-old Japanese woman who hails from Tokyo and enjoys karaoke. She Instagrams her meals and likes to play tabletop board games. But it is her work as an adult film star that has made her something of a symbol among younger Chinese who are pushing for more open and honest discussions of sexuality.

China is not known for being open about sexuality. Pornography is banned, sex work is illegal, the media is highly censored, and conservative opinions about gender roles and promiscuity remain widespread. So how on earth did a porn star like Aoi become a household name?

It all started on Twitter. Chinese users began to follow her there (where she tweets prolifically), and, recognizing the new influx of support from China, Aoi opened a Weibo account. Though it was rumored that China's censorship authorities banned her from appearing on television programs in 2012, she still managed to garner 14 million followers on Weibo.[36] This following not only makes her the most popular Japanese person in China by far, it also puts her among the top 100 social-media users in the entire country. After a couple of years on Weibo, Aoi is enjoying a "second spring" in the mainland, where she has landed lucrative endorsement deals, appeared on the cover of magazines, and held a successful singing concert.

It is not just her presence in China, but her engagement with Chinese fans that has propelled Aoi to such heights. As she moved away from Japanese adult films and into mainstream television and video work throughout Asia, Aoi reached out to her Chinese fan base and interacted with them. She started to learn Chinese and travel to China. The closer she has gotten to her fans, the more devoted they have become to her. To many in China, Aoi is more than just a porn star – she is a symbol of something lacking in Chinese society.

"Teacher Aoi," as she is called, is not an entirely ironic nickname. Many Chinese see Aoi's videos as instructional materials of a sort, filling in the gaps of China's sex education, which is, by the accounting of one Chinese academic, 60 years behind developed countries like Sweden. While Chinese authorities mandate sex education in theory, there is no national curriculum and the regulation is unevenly enforced.[37] Teachers are often uncomfortable with such taboo topics, and in the scramble to fit in all the instruction they can for students preparing to take China's national higher-education entrance exam (one of the world's most competitive tests) sex education easily falls by the wayside. In the absence of formal sex education, some high-school and college students have circulated the works of Sola Aoi among themselves and found them highly instructive.

As both a teacher and student, Sola has been a huge success in China. And that success says just as much about changes in Chinese society as it does about Aoi's own work ethic. As China has become a market economy, the more puritanical socialist society of the 1960s and 1970s has liberalized. Young people have far greater access to sexually explicit materials than ever before: On the internet, and even on television, clothes have become more revealing and dialogue more open. According to prominent Chinese sexologist Li Yinhe, in 1989, 15 percent of Chinese admitted to having premarital sex – most with partners they intended to marry – while in 2012, the figure had jumped to 71 percent.[38]

Aoi's social-media success has shown that there is a demand for greater sexual openness in China. Many have gone from secretly sharing files to openly proclaiming their fandom online. And this rapid opening-up online has further proven the power web users have wielded to challenge long-entrenched norms. As a rallying point, the Aoi-centered internet community has fought against sexual taboos in ways that simply could not have happened in mainstream media.

Out of the closet, onto the web

China's LGBT community has also fought against taboos on the internet. Gay-rights activists there were among the first to use social media to spread information about events, initiatives, and sex education. Because censorship authorities would not allow shows or films with LGBT characters on television or the silver screen, filmmakers and writers would distribute such content online. But the side effect of this marginalization was a flourishing of LGBT communities online – a cultural shift that in turn impacted all of China's internet users.

In China, as in most countries, LGBT individuals face a lot of pressure to conform to mainstream ideas of what is "normal." In a survey by Aibai, a Chinese gay-rights non-profit, more than 90 percent of respondents said they would remain closeted in the workplace, likely fearing that coming out would mean an end to their careers.[39] China has made no law protecting gay rights, let alone legalizing gay marriage. Homosexuality was not decriminalized until 1997, and it was officially considered a mental illness until 2001.[40]

But in recent years, attitudes toward homosexuality in China, especially among young people, have shifted considerably. This is apparent on Weibo, where users have supported and even encouraged openly gay individuals. As the platform grew in popularity, it appeared to be a somewhat more tolerant space than offline mainstream society.

In April 2012, this was put to the test. Famous Hong Kong singer Anthony Wong came out at a concert in front of thousands of fans, and the news went viral on Chinese social media. The 49-year-old Wong got a warm reception on Weibo, where "Anthony Wong announces he's coming out of the closet" became the number-one trending topic for that 24-hour period. Many wished him well, congratulated him, or took the opportunity to comment that attitudes on homosexuality had changed in recent years. In a survey conducted by Sina about the reaction to Wong's announcement, 47.8 percent of the 16,900 respondents said that Wong "was true to his feelings, and brave," while 19.3 percent said that they "could accept homosexuality, which is very common now." The remaining respondents either did not care (14.8 percent), or understood (13.1 percent). Only 5 percent were "surprised and confused that he felt the need to make it public."[41]

Of course, it has been easier for many to accept a stranger coming out than it has been to accept it of those they know. Many in China, both online and off, fell somewhere between begrudging acceptance of homosexuality in the abstract and active support of it in concrete instances.[42] The cost of posting about LGBT issues from an account your immediate social circle does not know about is low, compared to the cost some might face if they brought the issue up at the workplace or at home.

Wedding bells

Still, Chinese have continued to come out, protest for gay rights, and offer support for each other. In 2012, two Chinese men celebrated Qixi, the traditional Chinese equivalent of Valentine's Day, by announcing their engagement. "Zhong

Shao" and "Qiang Shao" posted their engagement pictures on Weibo, drawing hundreds of comments congratulating the pair and wishing them well. Through social-media coverage, they were able to find a venue to host their wedding ceremony.[43]

Such freedom isn't just for the young. In January 2013, two elderly men living in Beijing – who went by Mr. Yang and Mr. He – announced on Weibo that they, too, were going to get married. One was a retired professor, another was a migrant worker who met him while delivering water to his home. Most of those who commented on their posts voiced support for the union.[44] A gay-friendly alcohol distributor provided the liquor for their ceremony, a restaurant let them hold it in their venue for free, and a video website offered them a European honeymoon. The two men also thanked their Sina Weibo followers and popular gay portal website Danlan Online for their support and help.[45]

Many of their posts went viral, the most popular garnering 12,000 reposts and thousands of comments – enough to make it one of the most-read posts of the day. They live-streamed their wedding ceremony (until it was interrupted by their angry son) and defended their decisions to a sizeable audience of more than 14,000 Weibo followers. Danlan interviewed Mr. Yang on the occasion of their wedding. When asked if the two would persevere in spite of family disapproval, Yang said they would. "We'll keep going," he said. "If you're in love, you should persevere till the very end."[46]

New sites like Weibo have helped LGBT individuals in China connect with and support each other. Months before Danlan covered the Yang–He wedding, they had released an app called Blued, China's answer to Grindr.[47] Blued allows users to search for other gay men by proximity, much like the Chinese apps Momo and WeChat, and has chat and video features. In the first year, Blued drew more than 2 million users – a remarkable achievement for such a short period of time – and claimed more than 15 million as of 2014. What's more, Blued claimed that nearly a quarter of its users – 500,000 – logged on daily, compared to about a million on Grindr, which is the most established gay hookup app worldwide.[48]

As social media has allowed gay Chinese to find online support and connection, it has also revealed shifts in attitudes toward homosexuality among the larger internet population. On February 25, 2013, the organization Parents and Friends of Lesbians and Gays of China (PFLAG China) wrote an open letter to the country's National People's Congress, which was set to convene the next month, urging the legislators to revise China's marriage law so that their sons and daughters could enjoy the benefits of the institution. The letter went viral on Weibo, and Sina initiated an online poll in response, asking netizens: "How do you feel about PFLAG China's call to change the marriage law?" Of the approximately 74,000 respondents – quite high for a Weibo poll – 52.9 percent voted "I support it: Everyone should be able to love regardless of gender." Only 24.5 expressed explicit opposition, with the remaining respondents saying they would "neither support nor oppose" or "were not sure."[49]

Even Xinhua acknowledged that homosexuality is becoming less and less taboo, naming Qixi (China's Valentine's) "Gay Day" in an article about gay couples kissing in public on the holiday, in cities like Beijing, to take a stand for gay rights. The official news agency of China also attested that the number of gay-rights organizations, like PFLAG China, had "increased sharply" over the past five years.[50]

This trend would be far less pronounced if not for social media, where LGBT Chinese have been able to network, share resources, and realize they are not alone. On Weibo, these changes took place out in the open, chipping away at heteronormativity one post at a time.

A study in slash

China's increasing openness and willingness to talk about homosexuality has not remained confined to the internet – it's begun to make its way into television, for audiences in the hundreds of millions. In 2013, CCTV's Spring Festival Gala, which is watched by well over half a billion Chinese, surprised audiences when one of the hosts jokingly implied that two of the male performers, pop star Wang Leehom and famous pianist Li Yundi, were together.

The joke itself was a one-liner. As pianist Li Yundi peeked his head out of the curtain during the program, host Lu Chen asked him: "Who are you looking for? Leehom?" But the ostensibly off-the-cuff remark referenced a semi-serious rumor, one that had floated around the internet for years, that Li and Wang were an item. At a New Year's Eve concert at the end of 2012, fans had shouted "Get together" as the two shared the stage.[51] After the concert, Wang took to Weibo (where he has more than 41 million followers and is one of the site's most popular users) and made a statement: "I am straight, and Li Yundi also likes girls," he wrote. "What is the deal with all this 'Homdi' business?" His defense, referencing the "Brangelina"-like portmanteau fans had developed for the two, was reposted a whopping 248,000 times, making it far and away the most popular topic on Weibo that week.

Both Li and Wang have repeatedly denied they were boyfriend and boyfriend. In fact, on November 27, 2013, both musicians announced on social media that they had girlfriends. Wang's Weibo post to the effect has been reposted more than 993,000 times to date, while Li's garnered a not unimpressive 286,000.[52] (For context, Twitter's most shared tweets of 2013 all hovered around 400,000, while President Obama's victory tweet has amassed only about 765,000 as of late 2014.) The 575,000 comments left on Wang's and Li's posts included quite a few urging Li and Wang to kiss and make up. Their imagined romance remains a popular topic of discussion among internet users.

In China, the Homdi craze has coincided with a marked increase in the popularity of slash – that is, fanfiction depicting gay relationships between fictional characters. The Homdi phenomenon is essentially pop-culture slash, a romance with a life of its own (despite, or perhaps because of, the main characters' denial). But Chinese slash is by no means limited to wishes that Wang and Li would tie the knot. The genre covers everything from fanfic inspired by the BBC's *Sherlock* to original stories that have drawn large, paying readerships.

Once taboo, slash stories, particularly fanfic, have become incredibly popular in certain corners of the Chinese web. The rising tide is part of a cultural shift toward not just tolerance, but an embrace of counterculture and narratives that exist beyond the mainstream.

Where did all of this come from? It's safe to say that men have been kissing men, and women kissing women, since long before we started writing about any of it. But slash experienced something of a renaissance in the twentieth century. In fact, the word "slash" likely originated in the 1970s, when fans of the television show *Star Trek* began to circulate erotica featuring two of the series' male characters, Captain Kirk and Mr. Spock. They labeled the stories Kirk/Spock (Kirk-slash-Spock), and eventually the slash between them came to represent the same-sex love – and lust – described by their fans.

As slash was taking off in the United States, fiction about same-sex love was also sweeping another nation – Japan. Despite historical enmities, China has long turned to Japan for cultural imports like fashion trends and pop music, and erotica was no exception. After internet penetration started to rise in mainland China in the late 1990s, young Chinese began translating and reading Japanese fiction online. In part because of this influence, the Chinese word for slash is *danmei*, a Japanese loanword.

China draws influence from Japan and the United States (among other countries) but the online community that has risen around *danmei* is distinctly Chinese. For one thing, Weibo plays a large role in community building and the sharing of content. Abroad, Tumblr has become the beating heart of many of these fandoms and communities, but like Twitter, the site is blocked in China. Yet Weibo, like Tumblr, allows users to share gifs, embed video clips, and post multiple pictures at once. In addition, the 140-character limit allows for plenty of discussion in Chinese, much more than is possible in 140 letters from the Roman alphabet. The conversations that take place in Tumblr through reblogging with commentary flourish on Weibo as well.

Chinese slash has always been more internet-centric than its counterparts abroad because of censorship laws. China's traditional publishing apparatus is state-controlled, and the state has more rigid ideas about what sort of content is acceptable for publication. Because of this disparity, the

Chinese community that produces and consumes *danmei* is firmly bound to social media.

Slash fanfic based on foreign books, television shows, and movies is surprisingly visible on Weibo, where accounts established to repost and share gay erotica exist without much interference at all. Many Weibo users link to slash or post content online semi-anonymously (real-name registration requires users to submit their identification, but not display it publicly), which allows those who would be wary of public disapproval to enjoy fandom relatively free of worry.

There are also accounts for slash fans in particular cities, including Shanghai, Guangzhou, and Wuhan. These community hubs post information about group activities like movie viewings and book signings. A number of accounts dedicated to *danmei* literature have hundreds of thousands of followers on Weibo, while one has more than a million.[53] That account, @DanmeiFanficResources, shares comics translated from Japanese as well as pictures of the British actor Benedict Cumberbatch, star of *Sherlock*, short stories, and gifs.[54] It posts embedded videos about gay romance, clips that would likely never make it in the strictly regulated world of Chinese television.

[REDACTED]

Chinese authorities keep a close hold on domestic television and rarely allow foreign shows at all, much less those with subversive or explicit content. They also regularly issue new restrictions to limit "vulgar" content that might "negatively impact" the mental health of the country's young people.[55] The country's censorship ministry – known by the slimy mouthful of an acronym SAPPRFT – is vague about what constitutes "vulgar" content, but has axed shows in the past for violence, sex, or detailed depictions of criminal activity. Despite the Chinese government's repeated professions that internet censorship is necessary to curb pornography, explicit material seems less likely to meet the ax than calls for political protest.

In 2012, SAPPRFT cut back on entertainment programming, including reality shows aired on television.[56] In 2013, they moved to ban foreign shows from prime time and limit the number of episodes of a foreign series that might be broadcast in China.[57] The same year, singing competitions came under fire for their extravagance, sensationalism, and glitzy packaging. Authorities decreed that some would be postponed and rescheduled to avoid all of the singing programs airing at once.[58]

Directors in China have long complained that censorship authorities act in a slow, capricious manner, often pulling the plug on a production shortly before it is set to air.[59] Even television shows that have already been filmed have been canceled before they even had a chance to air, to the ire of networks that have invested their time and money creating them.[60] The pressure has led some directors to work abroad, and others to air their grievances with the state publicly.

In part, the rage directed at China's censorship bureau is due to the massive strain under which it operates: A bureaucratic organization, however massive, is ill equipped to go over the entertainment content for a country of 1.3 billion with a fine-toothed comb. But the lack of transparency involved in the process, as well as its unpredictability, also frustrate China's creative class.

Online, content producers have often found that it is easier to ask for forgiveness than permission. In theory, SAPPRFT controls the web just as firmly as it controls television stations, but it is already overstretched with traditional media, and has far less experience with the internet. The lower barriers to entry and quicker production period also open the playing field to a wider range of producers: Both individuals with camera phones and massive tech companies have published viral videos (and made money from ad revenues) on new web-based platforms.

The more Chinese authorities restrict traditional media like television, the more online media has become a necessary space for those who want to explore ideas beyond the closely controlled mainstream. Weibo in particular has become a hub connecting users who create and consume content that might otherwise never exist. The growing tendency to go online for entertainment content, instead of watching regular television or reading legally published books, has boosted the popularity and legitimacy of *danmei* as a genre as well.

But it's not all beer and skittles. Slash fiction is not just countercultural in China, it is also illegal, at least according to some Chinese law enforcement. In 2011, police in inland Henan province arrested a man who ran a website called Danmei Novels Online, charging that the site hosted more than 1,000 "sexually explicit" stories about gay men in relationships. State-run media called the genre a "harmful trend" and alleged that it would warp the minds of young girls, who seemed to be the main audience for the site, as well as the producers of most of its content.[61]

Another crackdown took place in April 2014. Police arrested the owner of a *danmei* website, as well as around 20 women who wrote for it, in an effort to "clean up" the web. A camera crew followed police to the houses of these girls – most of whom were around 20 years old – and the program played menacing music in the background as news anchors described *danmei* literature as illicit and lewd. Yet those interviewed by the police and news crew were less condemnatory. A number noted that similar content existed across the web, and that there didn't seem to be much wrong with it. "Online novels, pictures, and other stuff can get close to the line," said the site's founder from behind bars. "It's easy for them to get close to the line and a lot of them do."[62]

Slash fanfic may be considered "over the line" by authorities, but it's a world that most Chinese netizens both acknowledge and tolerate. It is a contained diversion from the norm. It is a rejection of the idea that heterosexual love is the best or most pure, challenging heteronormativity. It's both safe and dangerous. It shows solidarity with gay men at the level of consumption, without necessarily spilling over into one's public life.

Danmei might seem to be a niche genre with obvious appeal to gay men, but many of the most visible consumers and producers are in fact heterosexual young women. Women who consume slash erotica call themselves *funü*, which means "rotten girls," taken from the Japanese *fujoshi*, which has the same meaning but is also a homophone for "respectable woman." Why straight women? In truth, the phenomenon defies easy explanation. For *funü*, desire itself is enough. The idea that an affinity for slash fanfic is legitimate without logical justification pervades the community, which focuses on enjoyment rather than argument. They use the internet to share content, assert their right to be "perverts" and "rotten women," and connect with each other, largely ignoring or actively blocking out other netizens who would criticize their choices.

These women, and other fans of *danmei*, have not kept quiet and stayed in their corner of the internet. On Weibo and other platforms, they have made significant contributions to Chinese pop culture and have worked to destigmatize depictions of gay love in film and literature.

Elementary, my dear, dear Watson

One of the strongest *danmei* fan bases on the Chinese internet is that built around the BBC's *Sherlock*, a reimagining of Sir Arthur Conan Doyle's detective stories, set in the present day. *Sherlock* is big in China, so big that it was one of the first British shows to stream legally on the Chinese internet. Internet powerhouse Youku bought the rights to broadcast it for Chinese audiences in 2013, so that Chinese viewers could watch the show – with subtitles – just hours after it aired in Britain.[63]

The Holmes stories have been popular in China since not long after Doyle set them to paper. China's *Current Affairs Newspaper* published four of the stories in translation in 1896, and, in 1916, Zhonghua Book Company published the first translation of a collection of Holmes stories in Chinese, volumes that were reprinted more than 20 times in 20 years.[64] But it's hard to underestimate the new life breathed into Sherlock Holmes fandom by the 2010 BBC version. Benedict Cumberbatch, the show's star, has been key. One Chinese researcher has called the role he's played in boosting Chinese interest in British television "the *Sherlock* effect."[65] Cumberbatch has become a sex symbol worldwide, and China is no exception.

In China, Cumberbatch's fans often call him "Curly Fu." Sherlock Holmes has long been known in Chinese as "Fu'ermosi," a transliteration of Holmes, and since Cumberbatch came to play the role of the beloved detective, netizens named him "Curly Fu" because of his signature hairstyle. Doctor John Watson, whose last name is rendered phonetically as "Huasheng," is known as "Peanut," which is also pronounced *huasheng* in Chinese.

(Nicknames like this often blur the actor and character. For example, in Chinese discussions of the Marvel universe, Chris Hemsworth's Thor is known as "Chui Ge," "Brother Hammer," but Loki is "Dou Sen," a shortened transliteration of the actor Tom Hiddleston's last name. The slash pairing of Loki and Thor is also immensely popular, as are other Marvel pairings.)

A number of Weibo accounts dedicated to the Curly Fu/Peanut pairing have followers in the thousands.[66] One even links to a Taobao account that sells *Sherlock*-related goods, including a traditional Chinese New Year decoration featuring Cumberbatch's face.[67] MTSlash, a forum dedicated to Chinese-language slash fiction with more than 280,000 registered users, also has a Weibo account with more than 20,000 followers, where it updates about new content and activities.[68]

Chinese slash fanfic based on foreign content has several draws: It's removed enough from mainstream Chinese literature and art that the subversiveness of imagined gay romance draws less backlash from society at large. There's also a wealth of content already circulating online, ready for translation. Thousands of English-language slash stories, if not more, have been translated into Chinese for domestic consumption, both with the original author's permission and without.

Slash has, without a doubt, made an impact on modern Chinese culture. It has gone from guilty pleasure in hidden corners of the web to a prominent topic of discussion in the online public square. It is not universally liked or supported, but the community that creates it has already claimed the right to exist and thrive in public ways – both online and off.

While legal reform is still a distant possibility, social media has helped push forward cultural acceptance and understanding of LGBT issues is growing in China. And this growing tolerance is part of a larger set of culture shifts in commonly held beliefs, ethics, expectations, and identities that are changing everything.

—four—

NOT IN MY BACKYARD: FROM SCREENS TO STREETS

As we have seen, Chinese society is growing more tolerant and more cohesive. People are questioning age-old beliefs, cultural norms, and entrenched ideologies. But how do these changes play out in day-to-day life? When and why do things boil over? And what happens when new values collide with old realities?

The answer isn't simple. Sometimes collisions result in mass protests. Thousands, or even tens of thousands take to the street to demand changes they might have quietly accepted years ago. Other times, clashes between the old and new may only produce snide chatter online, the merciless dissection of outdated political ideology by keyboard warriors with no intention of setting foot outside. But even such mild forms of protest are having an impact on the way mainstream Chinese society grapples with its own discontent. What's more, the persons and groups that carry out these protests are incredibly diverse in almost every imaginable category. China's social web has become, as Professor Guobin Yang wrote in 2011, "an increasingly plural field of aspiring individuals and collectivities, sensibilities, associational forms, and practices."[1]

The following chapter explores three flashpoints – patriotism, pollution, and press freedom – and looks at the protesters they have inspired to take action. Each is a subject on which established institutions and significant segments of Chinese society have been slowly growing apart for years. And as the distance has grown greater, the discontent with top-down measures undertaken by the government and other power-ful organizations has grown stronger, often culminating in outbursts of unrest that have frightened those in charge – and even surprised the protesters themselves.

Not on my bookshelf: pushing back against "brainwashing" education

The Chinese government and the average Chinese person have very different ideas about the purpose of education. For most ordinary Chinese, education represents one of the few viable avenues of upward mobility. Study hard, and you might be able to get a decent job and buy a home one day. Chinese culture has also long prized learning: Teachers com-mand more respect in China than in many other countries, and families often make great sacrifices for their children's education.

The government, though it likely shares this sentiment, also sees education as a means to a political end. Educational materials are explicitly required to instill a love of the country and Party, and narratives of history are heavily tailored to that end. In some of the more extreme incidents, teachers staged a mock military operation in which students carried toy guns to go to war against Japan over disputed territory – in kindergarten.[2] Obviously, quality education still exists in China, but time spent on indoctrination is time taken from the nurturing of critical-thinking skills.

For these reasons, decisions about educational curricula can be quite political in China. In 2013, one such controversial decision made waves as China's People's Education Press, which produces many of the textbooks used by public schools, removed an essay from the latest edition of its textbooks. The essay in question was by Lu Xun (also written Lu Hsun), a man widely considered the father of modern Chinese literature but also feared for his sometimes subversive ideas.

Lu Xun's essays had been disappearing from official textbooks for years, with some arguing that the trend was simply a transition to more modern works. The language in many of his essays and stories, which were composed nearly a century ago, differs somewhat from the Chinese spoken and written today, so educators and students alike have complained that they are difficult to read.

But there may have been another reason authorities have been phasing him out. On the surface he doesn't seem so threatening – he's dead, after all, and he was a short, unimposing man even when he was alive. But his impact on China was profound. Heavily involved in the country's political and cultural movements in the early twentieth century, he mentored a generation of writers and activists who would shape China's future for decades after he passed.

He was also the harshest, sharpest and most snide of critics – he lived to make life miserable for his haters: "The reason I've quit drinking and started eating cod liver oil in order to extend my life isn't just for my wife, but also, and even mostly, for my enemies," he wrote in a collection of essays called *The Grave*, published in 1929. "Well anyway, 'enemies' is a nice way of putting it. I want to leave a few more flaws in their 'perfect world.'" The extent of his commitment to criticism was such that in his later years he turned away from short stories and published mainly collections of absolutely venomous essays. Lu Xun's works, written in the turmoil of an earlier China in which multiple political parties and nations competed for power, encouraged readers to question authority and think for themselves, sharply attacking outdated traditions, rigid dogmas, and overly ideological mindsets. Even today, a century later, his rhetoric about wishful thinking, unquestioning subservience, and hypocrisy heavily influences debate in China about politics. Online polls reveal that Chinese overwhelmingly feel Lu Xun is a critical part of China's literary history and that his stories should remain in schools.

Some see the phasing out of Lu Xun as a part of a long project that ensures schools teach loyalty to the Party first and independent thinking second, if at all.[3] China's state news agency did little to dispel the notion that the curricula decision was partly an ideological one. Xinhua promoted a local paper's article on the subject, quoting an expert who explained that Lu Xun's works were "too deep." Another author quoted by the article argued: "We shouldn't make students undertake reflection and critical thinking too soon; instead, we should let them gradually accumulate knowledge."[4]

This is not the first time that the politics of education has made waves on social media in China. In July 2013, China's Ministry of Education – together with Party and propaganda authorities – released a list of 100 books and 100 movies and shows that they planned to push on China's children. The list was explicitly designed to "promote the national spirit" and encourage youth to fight for "the great rejuvenation of the Chinese nation."

What was on the list? *Stories of Marx. Never Forget National Humiliation. Flowers of the Motherland.* There were a few offerings that had little to do with politics, like a book on geography, but most were quite red indeed. Online, there was a severe and immediate backlash against the list. Some parents said they would consider home-schooling. Others wrote that they would keep the list handy as a reminder of "what not to read." On a more snide note, some hinted that they would rather use the books as toilet paper than read them: "When are you sending over the books?" one Weibo user asked. "Make sure the paper is very soft please!"[5]

But it didn't stop at mockery. Users shared books they recommended that had not made the list, including *Charlotte's Web* and *Cinderella*. And the whole fiasco was negative publicity for China's Ministry of Education, which came off looking out of touch. It had been decades since China forbade foreign literature, and the increasing openness had left many without much of a taste for heavy-handed political texts.

In the era of Weibo, opposition to top-down decisions about children's education could gain momentum that might otherwise remain as isolated grumbling. The Ministry of Education might – and probably will – continue to do as it planned, but parents would feel more confident telling children to think for themselves, knowing that many other parents would do the same.

Later in the same year, the People's Education Press sparked even more debate by putting out a language and literature textbook containing six errors. To make matters worse, the publisher did not even apologize until pressed – and then sued – by a teacher angry that it refused to acknowledge the errors publicly. When the suit became widely known, the press only issued an apology on its own website, not in a media statement. Furthermore, it refused to recall the textbooks or even contact schools to inform them of the errors, agreeing only to correct the mistakes in future editions.[6]

Peng Banghuai, the teacher who has sued the publishing house over the errors, said that this was not unusual in his experience. He said he had found other errors in previous years and run up against a brick wall when he attempted to inform the publishers. He had mailed his findings but received no response. When he called, they stated they had received the letter and were processing the changes. But in the next year's revised edition, the errors were still there.[7]

Debate about the official publishing house's handling of textbook errors revealed deeper problems: On Weibo, many argued that the heavily political and restricted process for textbook composition led to such errors, as only a few people were allowed to participate and private competition was not allowed. What began as anger about the potential for incorrect instruction led, as many issues in China do, to dissatisfaction with authorities over their monopolization and mishandling of important tasks.

The publisher's response fueled this dissatisfaction. By all accounts, the way that it handled the fiasco was a good example of what not to do: refusing to admit an error until it became impossible to keep it quiet, and then making only as many concessions as necessary to get by. Yet this method of handling unpleasant truths is not unfamiliar to many Chinese: It has reared its head in any number of crises, including the aftermath of the Sichuan earthquake and the Wenzhou train crash. In this case and in most others, the reluctant, half-hearted way of addressing important matters has only reinforced public suspicion that authorities' first priority is preserving power, not handling problems. Incidents like this have continued to harm the credibility of China's government bodies and the institutions associated with them.

"Patriotic" or propaganda?

Educational curricula are an even more sensitive political issue in Hong Kong, which has had trouble accepting classroom changes that have occurred in the past few years. Beginning in 2010, bureaucrats in Hong Kong began trying to replace the city's existing "moral and civic education" curricula with "moral and national education," which was more politically biased toward the China model. After testing the waters in 2011, the education bureau attempted to roll out the revised curricula in some schools in the summer of 2012, to massive public opposition.

Hong Kong residents, already upset over a decline in free-dom of the press since Britain returned the city to China in 1997, took to the streets to voice their displeasure over what they termed "brainwashing education." They rejected the new materials, which were critical of the United States' two-party system and called the CCP "an advanced, selfless and united ruling group."[8]

Tens of thousands protested that July, and the number swelled to more than 100,000 as resistance to the changes increased. Students formed a group called Scholarism to oppose the curricula, and parents formed the National Education Parents' Concern Group. Both groups, but particu-larly Scholarism, used social-media sites like Facebook (which is not censored in Hong Kong) to organize and publicize pro-tests. In August, Scholarism began to occupy the public park in front of government headquarters, and some began a hunger strike. Hong Kong protesters even employed the "grass-mud horse" meme to criticize the Party.[9] "We don't want the next generation of Hong Kong people to be brainwashed," Joshua Wong, the then 15-year-old co-founder of Scholarism, told

CNN.[10] Ultimately, Hong Kong administrators backed off, saying that they would let schools decide whether or not to use the new teaching materials. Protesters exited the park, cleaning up the trash on their way out, and most considered the result a victory. This was not the final battle for Scholarism or any of the other groups that had formed in reaction to perceived encroachment by Beijing. They formed connections and discussion groups, and organized on a number of issues, including universal suffrage and freedom of expression. Still, they were a small group, an assortment of politicians and student activists meeting on occasion, their numbers diminished significantly by the resolution of the curriculum controversy.

But all of that changed in the summer of 2014. Beijing announced new stipulations for the elections in 2017, the year it had promised Hong Kong could hold a democratic vote for its leadership. The people of Hong Kong would still get to cast their ballots, but Beijing would, through the city's legislative committee, effectively vet the candidates and explicitly require any potential candidate to "love the country." Most of Hong Kong's democracy advocates felt that this provision castrated the process entirely, leaving only the illusion of choice.

Once again, Hong Kong's politicians and student activists rallied. They conducted surveys, researched possible compromises, submitted proposals, and called for discussions. But when those in power would not listen, they began to employ the tactics of civil disobedience. The students went on strike, and a democracy activist named Benny Tai proposed that everyone occupy Central, the business district, where Hong Kong's government offices are located.

On September 28, they began to do just that. Activists convened in Central, where they held up signs in peaceful protest. Thousands of them sat peacefully, singing songs and listening to speeches by the organizers. But the peace was short-lived. Later that evening, police attempted to clear the area with tear gas, pepper spray, and batons.

The protesters were shocked – such measures had not been taken for almost a decade in the city – but instead of lashing out violently, they dug in their heels and made it clear they would not be moved. Umbrellas, face masks, and goggles began to circulate through the crowds. Where police fired tear gas, the protesters held up umbrellas of every color imaginable as shields. And in other neighborhoods throughout the city, people began to assemble spontaneously in solidarity with the protesters at Central. Instead of scaring people into submission, the violent tactics of the riot police caused the protest's numbers to swell dramatically.

By the next day, protesters were in high gear. One participant described the atmosphere:

At five o'clock, students arrived in their uniforms, carrying their book bags. At seven, professionals came in their business attire and their high heels. At nine, young people, ethnic minorities who grew up in Hong Kong and spoke fluent Cantonese, arrived on the scene to proclaim their support for the peaceful movement. Around eleven, tattooed punks began to arrive by motorcycle and delivery truck, unloading material goods to help those gathered there. Such a spontaneous outpouring of mutual aid was unprecedented in Hong Kong, and brought rounds of applause as well as tears as protesters welcomed the selfless donations from people of all walks of life, and everyone put aside their disagreements and differences. On that night, a feeling of peace truly suffused the over 100,000 Hong Kongers who had joined together.[11]

The sit-ins, sleep-ins, barricades, and strikes continued through the next week – and China's National Day. Students were able to draw concessions from the government in the form of talks with Hong Kong's central leadership.

This sudden surge of resistance did not appear fully formed from the void. Discontent with the status quo and hope for something much more had been fermenting in Hong Kong for years, and the freedom of expression, uncensored internet, and strong press environment had only accelerated their growth. Rising anti-mainland sentiment – many in Hong Kong were upset that Chinese from across the border were putting a strain on the city's hospitals and pricing locals out of apartments – further fueled the flames. But mass protests only happened when Beijing acted as it had always done on the mainland, either unwilling or unable to see that Hong Kong had become incapable of tolerating such treatment.

In short, the Occupy movement in Hong Kong was what happened when people reached breaking point. Slow shifts that took place over decades laid the groundwork, but when police used violent tactics to clear protesters, the large demonstrations gained staying power. What happens next is not clear – but what has already happened has revealed that the unrest over changes in Hong Kong so far is only the tip of the iceberg.

Pollution: the smog that broke the camel's back

Though not quite as sexy as battles over democracy, disputes over pollution in China's air and water have also grown more politically significant in recent years. In 2013, environmental concerns replaced land disputes as the main cause of "mass incidents," a euphemism for protests.[12] Data is unsurprisingly hard to come by, but China sees tens of thousands of protests a year, and, since 2012, a growing number have been Not in My Backyard (Nimby) protests against plants and factories that locals worry will negatively impact their immediate environments and potentially their own health.

They have good reason to worry: Even China's state-run media has acknowledged the existence of "cancer villages," localities where pollution from factories has led to sickness and death.[13] It has even killed the crops that villagers depend on to earn their living. "Nothing comes from these plants," a farmer in one rural cancer village told the *Wall Street Journal* last year. "They're actually dead inside."[14]

And these villages are not isolated occurrences: In fact, there are hundreds.[15] As the central government has pressured local bodies to achieve high levels of economic growth for decades, industrial regulation has too often fallen by the wayside. In the past, cancer villages existed mainly along China's highly developed eastern coast; now they are beginning to appear farther and farther inland.[16]

In Shaozhuang, a village so small that most people share a surname, cancer is everywhere. In 2004, one resident told a journalist that entire families were dying out: "Shao Heyu's family lost four people in two years," she said. "Their son Shao Haicheng was only 30. That's it for their family line. Shao Daoqun's family line has also been cut off. Those two families got liver cancer." Nearby Lihan Village fared no better. The top official in the village said that 18 had died in 2003, and 23 in 2004 – out of a total population of 2,000 or so: "Almost all of them had cancer," he said.[17]

Residents of these villages are increasingly aware that pollution is to blame for their ailments. Awareness of potential consequences has also risen in areas that have yet to be directly affected, weighting public opinion against proposed plants and factories that might decades ago have been welcomed for the jobs and investment they brought. Though protests against plants have taken place since at least 1997, they have escalated as information about industrial pollution's negative effects has spread, often through social networks like Weibo.

Two recent protests often cited as examples of the Nimby movement in China are those that took place in less central Chinese cities. In Shifang, a city in central Sichuan province, protesters came out in force against a molybdenum–copper alloy plant that they feared would pollute the environment and cause health problems.[18] "Save Shifang! All city residents unite!" exclaimed posters put up in the city calling on people to protest. "This is our shared home, and it is our responsibility to protect it [...] Once construction of the factory begins, it will already be too late."[19]

People did take to the streets, but riot police met the protesters and violently put down the demonstration, beating people until some had to be hospitalized. Graphic images circulated online: a man bleeding from the head in a hospital, another injured man walking away from the crowds with blood staining the front of his shirt, a woman crying while holding her young son.[20] Rumors that students had been beaten to death further stoked public outrage. The protest and its aftermath generated millions of posts on Weibo, thousands of which contained on-the-ground footage and pictures.[21] Local authorities quickly canceled the planned project to calm the situation.

In a small coastal city called Qidong locals marched against a proposed waste discharge plant in July of the same year. Afraid that the plant would pollute their local water supply, they ransacked the local-government building and posted pictures of the destruction online. In one particularly vivid picture that came out of the protest, a single protester stood with his back to the camera, facing a line of riot police.[22] Circulating on Weibo, this and other images resonated with many throughout China who felt the demands they made of their local governments often went unheard or unanswered. Authorities quickly responded by canceling the Qidong project.[23] "We are aware of the Shifang experience, and if it worked there then it may work here," one student protester there told Reuters, on the condition of anonymity. "We have a responsibility to protect our home."[24]

In 2013, similar protests took place in Kunming, Yunnan province; Jiangmen, Guangdong province; and Ningbo, Zhejiang province. Some even turned violent, with riot police using tear gas on protesters and beating them. But across China, citizens began offering support for their compatriots protesting for environmental safety. Even face masks worn on hazy days became symbols of resistance. Ultimately, many of these protests ended in authorities relenting, canceling plans, or promising to put projects on hold until they had generated sufficient public support.

These instances of appeasement became known to Chinese in other parts of the country through Weibo and other online platforms. Each instance of compromise showed people that public dissatisfaction would be answered, should it reach critical mass. And the bravery of protesters also inspired many who felt that public demonstration was a futile, dangerous pursuit. The odds are stacked against Chinese protesters,

especially in small towns where corporations and local officials wield tremendous power to ruin lives. But still they
have marched.

Weibo chatter about pollution over the years laid much
of the groundwork for these protests. Of course, dissatisfaction with smog or potential health hazards can exist
without the aid of social media, but the microblogging
platform helped spread knowledge and raise awareness of
the dangers.

Choking on smog: the Beijing blues

While protests like those in Shifang and Qidong were flashpoints, sudden surges of resistance, anti-pollution sentiment
has moved more slowly in China's capital, Beijing. Ever since
social media began to become popular there, residents of the
city would often upload pictures of Beijing's skyline, obscured
by a gray haze, and repost news stories about the canceled
flights and spikes in respiratory illnesses that resulted. The
smog that frequently cloaked Beijing and other major cities
embarrassed authorities, whose emphasis on development
before environmental regulation has contributed to the
unhealthy air there.

Discontent over Beijing's air pollution was on a low boil
for years, even decades, before it reached levels demanding
an official response. In the days before microblogging, most
residents of Beijing and other polluted urban areas may
have complained occasionally about the haze, but ultimately
accepted it as a part of life. Yet persistent coverage of the
phenomenon, as well as measurement of air quality over
time, made the everyday matter a point of contention for a
great number of people.

The US embassy in Beijing played a part in bringing the issue to the fore. The building, located in one of the more central areas of Beijing, monitored the levels of particulate matter smaller than 2.5 micrometers (PM 2.5), which is considered especially harmful. The embassy began tweeting PM 2.5 levels every hour, on a zero to 500 scale, in 2008. Eventually, US consulates in Shanghai and Guangzhou also began sharing this information.

Readings ranged from good (0–50), to moderate (51–100), to unhealthy for sensitive groups (101–150), to unhealthy (151–200), to very unhealthy (201–300), to hazardous (301–500). By checking a smartphone app or visiting a special website, Beijing residents could determine whether it was a good day for a run (moderate – get in some exercise!) or more suitable for staying indoors (hazardous – better kick back and watch a movie indoors).[25] At times, pollution in China's capital was bad enough that equipment was not capable of measuring it. In one such instance in 2010, the embassy tweeted that the air was "crazy bad," but in later readings, the embassy switched to the phrasing "beyond index."

The figures released by the US embassy in Beijing often diverged from China's officially reported numbers, in part because measurement methods differed. The embassy monitored PM 2.5 particles – which are on the increase – while Chinese measurement tools took stock of larger PM 10 particles (those between 2.5 and 10 micrometers) – which are decreasing. China's official sensors were also placed throughout the city, including in more remote areas, whereas the US embassy monitored pollution only in its own relatively central location. Though Twitter was blocked in China, the US embassy's readings frequently ended up on Weibo, through the help of prominent figures concerned with Beijing's air pollution, like real-estate mogul Pan Shiyi, a highly popular Weibo user with millions of followers. China's officials were not pleased with this trend.

As early as 2009, according to a WikiLeaks cable, Chinese diplomats had angrily demanded that the United States stop publishing air-pollution readings, but by 2012, they were an intolerable embarrassment. That year, a Chinese environmental ministry official publicly claimed that the United States' reporting of its own measurements was against both Chinese and international law, and demanded that the embassy cease and desist.[26]

But the embassy was determined to continue. Every hour, on the hour, it posted the information on its website and Twitter, just as China continued to post its own readings. As the sparring between the embassy and Chinese officials went public, so did the debate about air quality. Domestic media began to report on pollution, and it gained ground in the public consciousness. More people bought and wore face masks on polluted days. Almost everyone, from professors of environmental science to migrant workers newly arrived in Beijing, became aware of the danger posed by Beijing's heavy haze. The weather channel and press even began to use a new word, "smog," to describe the lowered visibility of the capital when pollution was high. In previous years, they had called the gray air "clouds" or "fog."

Pollution would inevitably have become a hot topic in Chinese society, but its shift into the spotlight was helped by coverage in the news and on social media. The participation of individuals, including celebrities and noted Chinese microbloggers like Pan Shiyi, was invaluable: Through their tweets on the subject, the issue was seen not just as foreign meddling in China's domestic affairs, but as a problem that concerned all residents of Beijing equally. As it became clear that the public was unwilling to let the issue of pollution drop, authorities shifted from censoring pollution-related posts to announcing measures to tackle Beijing's air-quality problems.

Beijing's smog is just one among many issues that Weibo users have tackled through collective action since the platform first became popular. In this instance, debate about the severity of the problem did not begin on Weibo, but it ended up there because of its relevance to the Chinese citizenry and the lack of coverage from traditional media (who were likely pressured not to pay too much attention to it). No other virtual space played so great a role as Weibo, not because of its unique features, but because it was the virtual equivalent of an urban public square. It was space, not content, that allowed dissatisfaction and demand for change to grow organically, eventually becoming too big for authorities to contain.

The *Southern Weekly* incident

Like pollution or patriotism, press freedom is a contentious issue in China – and it is also a dangerous one. The country's government relies on censorship and "public-opinion guidance" to create a stable political environment and smooth away obstacles to the exercise of power. Anything seen to be a viable threat to that – a large enough demonstration, or a single person speaking out with enough reach – will not be tolerated.

That's why a small protest for freedom of speech that took place in early 2013 is more significant than one might assume at first glance. The participants knew that, given the sensitivity of the timing and their demands, there could be very, very real consequences. In fact, two of the protest's participants were later detained for more than a year and then indicted on charges of "gathering crowds to disrupt order in a public place" for their actions that day.[27] If similar cases are any indication, they will likely spend years in prison.

But the story of this particular protest did not begin on the streets – it began in the editorial room of the *Southern Weekly*, a popular, liberal newspaper long considered China's most outspoken. At the beginning of each year, the weekly publishes a special "New Year's greeting" op-ed, looking back on events it has covered and forward to issues it feels will be important in the not-so-distant future. But the op-ed drafted for publication in 2013's first edition never reached the presses. In what many saw as an unprecedented encroachment on the paper's operations, local propaganda authorities forced the weekly to publish a different essay, containing a typo, incoherent wording, and historical inaccuracies, without the permission of the *Southern Weekly*'s editors.

The first proposed version of the New Year's greeting was entitled "The Chinese dream, the dream of constitutionalism."[28] It spoke of China's nascent constitutionalism movement, a push for enforcement of laws and guarantee of rights contained in China's existing constitution. "Only by realizing the dream of constitutionalism can we all dream our own individual dreams," wrote Dai Zhiyong, the commenter in charge of penning the piece. "So it must start from us; we must protect our lives at this point in time, not leave this heavy burden to our children and grandchildren."[29] But after weeks of back-and-forth between editors and censors, the weekly eventually published a dramatically different version entitled "Pursuing our dreams."

The "constitutionalism" referenced by Dai was, by early 2013, a rallying point for reform-minded Chinese. It first gained traction when it was included in Charter 08, a manifesto co-authored by Nobel Peace Prize winner Liu Xiaobo, as one of the fundamental concepts demanded by signatories. The charter defined constitutionalism as

> the principle of guaranteeing basic freedoms and rights of citizens as defined by the constitution through legal provisions and the rule of law, restricting and defining the boundaries of government power and conduct, and providing appropriate institutional capability to carry this out.[30]

The term gained even more momentum as national debate about rule of law heated up in 2011 and 2012.

Why was the "dream of constitutionalism" intolerable to authorities? On the surface, the term and movement it represented were far from radical, especially compared to other terms, like "democracy", that also appeared in Charter 08. But since constitutionalism seeks to place restraints on the state's power, those in power saw it as a direct threat to their own authority and legitimacy. Chinese authorities began to push back against proponents of constitutionalism in 2012, accusing them of being unpatriotic and corrupted by Western influences. Later in 2013, anti-constitutionalism gained strength as Party media announced that it was a wrong, subversive idea that originated in the West.[31]

So instead of Dai's essay on constitutionalism, readers picked up their January 3 New Year's issue of the *Southern Weekly* and found a short note lauding the dream of a "strong," "well-governed" and "happy" China. That dream "has never been closer than today, and therefore has never been more deserving of the tireless exploration and unceasing struggle of the country's people!" it declared, complete with exclamation marks. The brief essay, stripped of all controversial language, included such glaring errors – a typo, a historically inaccurate statement, and a sentence that did not even make sense – as to alert most readers to the sweeping last-minute changes that had been made.

After the issue hit stands, social-media users began to speculate that a propaganda official, not a member of the *Southern Weekly* staff, had written "Pursuing our dreams." Critics felt that the level of interference from propaganda and censorship officials was unacceptable.[32] Some of the weekly's staff leaked information to other media outlets about the struggle with censors, making it widely known on Weibo and other social-media platforms. As various members of the *Southern Weekly* staff posted the original New Year's greeting on Sina Weibo, it went viral. Mega-celebrities like Yao Chen and Chen Kun – at present the two most popular Weibo users, with 62 million and 71 million followers respectively, each far more popular than, say, President Obama is on Twitter – voiced support for the embattled media outlet with Weibo posts and reposts.[33] In the number-one trending Weibo post that day, with almost 100,000 reposts, Yao voiced support of the paper and freedom of speech by quoting Solzhenitsyn: "One word of truth outweighs the world."[34] All of this high-power support – and a curious lag on the part of Sina Weibo's censors – resulted in widespread knowledge of *Southern Weekly*'s struggle.

Days later, in hopes of dispelling the "rumors" that the published essay was written by a propaganda official, authorities demanded that *Southern Weekly* make a formal statement on the authorship of the New Year's greeting. They passed an order through the weekly's acting editor-in-chief, demanding that it publish a statement through its official Weibo account reading: "The January 3 New Year's Message and its introduction in the New Year's edition of this newspaper were written by editors at the paper in accordance with the theme of 'seeking dreams.'"[35]

Individuals resisted, even in the face of the inevitable. Wu Wei, the staff member in charge of the paper's Weibo account, refused to issue the notice outright. As his superiors transferred social-media responsibilities to another employee, Wu posted through the paper's official account that he was stepping aside and could "no longer take any responsibility for the content about to be posted or any content posted hereafter" – a damning comment that was censored almost immediately.[36] A short time later, around 9:30 at night, the controversial statement was finally published on Weibo.

Quite a few members of the *Southern Weekly* team disagreed with the decision, and said as much through their own Weibo accounts. The members of the paper's economics section signed a unanimous open letter declaring that "the statement made" by the *Southern Weekly* Weibo account "does not represent the stance of the *Southern Weekly* sourcing and editorial personnel. It is the result of pressure exerted upon management by the relevant bureau." The economics section staff avowed that they would "oppose the untrue statement to the very end" and would not work until the matter was resolved.[37]

The next day, the strike began. Crowds gathered outside the offices of the *Southern Weekly* in the southern city of Guangzhou, as activists, students, and ordinary individuals joined the staff of the paper in protest. Some held signs calling for democracy and human rights, others shouted slogans about press freedom. Many carried chrysanthemums, which symbolize mourning in China.[38] Almost everyone had a cellphone out and was actively uploading pictures to Weibo and WeChat. Authorities censored as fast as they could, but images still appeared, if fleetingly, on social media.

Police broke up the protest, loading up some of the demonstrators into vans, but the brief stand-off had ripple effects far beyond the *Southern Weekly* itself. Perhaps in hope of discouraging other papers from getting ideas, propaganda authorities required other news outlets to republish an editorial from the *Global Times* criticizing the *Southern Weekly*. The editorial called people protesting the *Southern Weekly* incident "extreme" and downplayed their unity by noting that they were "connected through the internet, but quite fragmented in reality." Noting that China "could not possibly" have the free media that the protesters were demanding, the editorial made the consequences of continued protest clear: "In China, people who do this will lose," it read. "Don't force a Chinese paper to perform the role of an opponent [of the system]; this is a role that it cannot possibly undertake."[39]

Across the country, papers that did comply with orders to repost the editorial on their websites added notes beneath it, reminding readers that "a repost does not mean an endorsement." Major online news aggregators such as Sina, NetEase, Ifeng, and Sohu all found creative ways to subtly voice support for the staff of the *Southern Weekly*. The *Beijing News*, another influential paper formerly owned by the same media conglomerate as the *Southern Weekly*, initially refused to publish the piece point-blank. By midnight of January 8, they were under pressure to repost on pain of the paper's dissolution, but the editorial staff present in the office unanimously voted not to do so. Dai Zigeng, the paper's publisher, even offered his resignation to authorities in protest over the matter. Eventually, the paper posted the editorial, but no one was willing to sign off on the editorial work for the article, and so the byline was left blank.[40]

The staff of the *Southern Weekly* went back to work, as did the employees of the *Beijing Times*. Censorship and subtle resistance once again reached equilibrium.[41] But the protests were not forgotten by those who had voiced their support, either on Weibo or by taking to the streets.

What the *Southern Weekly* incident made clear was this: Even with censorship committees in place within media outlets, even with laws in place forbidding the posting of certain kinds of content, even with decades of forced experience in self-censorship, China's domestic journalists, celebrities, and ordinary citizens can still be a wildcard for the Party. Liberal-leaning papers constantly push boundaries, and even the hard-line nationalist propaganda outlets are quicker to question decisions they feel unfair than they were decades ago. In decades past, many Chinese saw the CCP and its leaders as the country's moral center; now, the country's legitimacy is anchored to its legacy, a set of ideals and a historical narrative. Much like the term the "Chinese dream," that legacy is open to interpretation.

These days, more and more people are choosing narratives of China that do not align with the interests of the country's ruling party. Or perhaps these people feel that the interests of that party have slowly diverged from their own. Whatever is shifting – likely everything – China's new political landscape has become a minefield for those who, whether through their own ignorance or wishful thinking, remain stuck in the past.

five

I FOUGHT
THE LAW

When Americans talk about struggles in other countries, a word that pops up a lot is freedom – freedom of speech or freedom of assembly. But most of the time, activists in China struggle to promote more specific kinds of reform, or protest discrete incidents in which they were wronged. In her book *Now I Know Who My Comrades Are*, Emily Parker interviewed a blogger named He Caitou who said just that: "Chinese people don't care about freedom. But they do care about justice."[1] The statement was hyperbolic, certainly, but He has a point. Without personal experience and a feeling of investment, most people would be very unlikely to care much for something as abstract as freedom. This is especially true in China, where the concept of freedom has historically carried less weight than it has in countries with long-standing democracies.

This chapter explores how personal experiences with corruption in law enforcement, unresponsive courts, or economic pressure have propelled ordinary individuals to the forefront of the push for legal and political reform. Furthermore, it shows how Weibo and other social media have shown vast audiences how these individuals' experiences are part of larger issues in China. As the marginalized have begun to use social media to demand justice, they've changed not only their own circumstances, but society's conceptions of the present and hopes for the future.

Weibo and the court of public opinion

Weibo has become an arena for spectators of China's judicial system. In the past, trials were rarely publicized, with rare, political exceptions. Newspapers might report verdicts, but would seldom detail proceedings. Weibo has changed that. Media outlets, aware that Chinese are hungry for details and invested both in outcomes and processes, have pushed for as much access as they can obtain. When reporters are barred from the courts, journalists interview anyone willing to speak on the matter and share their findings. Weibo has become the platform where all of this information from all possible sources is pieced together, debated, and analyzed, placing China's judicial system under closer supervision than at any point in history.

The mother: Tang Hui

In most pictures, Tang Hui is looking away from the camera. A woman in her middle years, she wears her hair short and dresses plainly – for many years, she lived quietly with her husband in one of China's farther-flung cities, running a small business and helping to raise their daughter. But when their daughter – the couple's only child – went missing, Tang started down a long road toward justice, eventually becoming one of the most well-known people in a fight to clean up China's entire judicial system.

It was almost ten years ago, in October 2006, when Tang's 11-year-old child disappeared. The girl's mother looked everywhere, searching high and low in the city where she lived, Yongzhou, for three months. Finally, Tang received an anonymous tip-off after posting pictures of the girl online: She was in a brothel.

The 11-year-old had been raped repeatedly for three full months, and on at least one occasion by four men at the same time. When Tang discovered her daughter's whereabouts, she immediately went to the police, demanding an investigation. But the police refused to help. Tang took matters into her own hands, disguising herself as a cleaner in order to pass undetected near the building to look for signs of her daughter. When she finally spotted the young girl, Tang called several of her relatives and the local police and they forcibly removed her. A doctor who examined the girl said that she had post-traumatic stress disorder and had sustained serious harm.

It took days of calling before the police would agree to open a case. Even after they rescued Tang's daughter, they made no move to close down the brothel: "Don't tell me how to do my job," the police would tell her when she stopped by the station to ask about the investigation. The courts then appointed her public defenders, but they seemed uninterested in helping her, remarking that the girl did not seem to have been forced. "She doesn't seem like she's only 11," one told her.[2] It was only after Tang protested by kneeling in front of the court for 18 hours in a snowstorm that authorities agreed to appoint a new lawyer for her daughter's case.

Tang pushed for the trial. Then she pushed for harsher sentences for those involved in her daughter's suffering. Five of the men implicated received jail time, two of those who had gang-raped her and forced her into prostitution were sentenced to death, but the two police officers who initially refused to open the investigation and warned the brothel owner ahead of time to relocate the underage girls there received only warnings. At each turn, she fought delays, denials, and reluctance to follow through on the part of authorities.

After years of demanding justice, she began to stage more intrusive protests: She lay down in front of government officials' cars. She refused to leave the courtroom. In her desperation, she even threatened to commit suicide. She petitioned in Changsha, the capital of Hunan province, and then took her grievances to Beijing. When she reached the capital, the police decided she was "disturbing public order" and, on August 2, 2012, ordered that she undergo two years of "re-education through labor" – a "sentence" handed down without a trial.

The news that Tang was to spend two years in a labor camp generated an immediate backlash. She filed a suit against the authorities, and her lawyer contacted influential Weibo users like investigative journalist Deng Fei. Prominent writers and social critics stood up for Tang and demanded her release. Tens of thousands of Weibo users lashed out at the Yongzhou police, who released two statements on the social-media platform defending their decision and criticizing Tang.

For these Weibo users, Tang Hui was not just another woman – she was *shangfang mama*, "the petitioning mother." Petitioning is a millennia-old system in China, dating back to ancient times when ordinary people with grievances could take them to the local courts, or travel to the capital if they could not find justice at home. Legend has it that such systems existed as far back as the time of Emperor Yao, a mythical figure said to have reigned more than 4,000 years ago. Conjecture aside, history shows that petitioning was taking place in the Western Zhou Dynasty (1100–771 BCE), more or less during Europe's Iron Age. In later dynasties, Chinese would beat "grievance drums" as they recited their complaints.[3] As a petitioner, Tang called to mind Chinese throughout the ages who had stood up to powerful officials and demanded justice.

In modern China, the petitioning system was codified and made into an administrative bureau: the State Bureau for Letters and Calls. In theory, the bureau exists to amend failures of the political system: A wronged individual like Tang could complain to the local authorities or someone higher up the food chain, and those leaders would, in a perfect world, respond and see justice done. In practice, many problems these individuals have are with the local authorities, who have little incentive to punish themselves and even less to let petitioners carry word of their wrongdoings on to Beijing.

Furthermore, until very recently, local authorities would receive negative evaluations from their superiors – which would lower their chances of promotions and raises – if petitioners from their jurisdiction made it to Beijing. Supposedly, this was done to encourage lower-level bureaucrats to resolve petitioners' problems at the local level. But in reality, it led many local governments to forcibly prevent disgruntled citizens from carrying their complaints to the capital. Across China, "black jails" sprouted up to hold petitioners against their will and, in some cases, torture them.

Many Chinese think petitioners are crazy for going up against those more powerful than themselves, but petitioners' persistence in the face of all odds has also inspired sympathy and hope. They represent trust in the system, even when that system has wronged them, as well as a thirst for justice. Tang Hui, as a devoted mother and a tireless petitioner, inspired fierce loyalty among those who followed the case.

Tang's treatment also led many to question the re-education-through-labor system. The system, known by the shorthand of *laojiao*, was established in the early days of the People's Republic of China and used to punish counter-revolutionaries – which in practice was anyone whose thoughts or actions were deemed questionable by those in power. Since then, the camps have expanded in scope to accept prisoners who are deemed lazy, have frequented prostitutes, or have disrupted public order. Conditions can be harsh, and prisoners overworked. It is also not part of the larger justice system, and therefore governed by the public-security and justice bureaus directly: Police can send Chinese citizens to serve up to two years in the camps without even a trial. It is a convenient way for police or the courts to get rid of troublesome individuals without the fuss of due process. One Weibo user wrote of the system: "When ordinary people can lose freedom or even life at the whim of one official, where is the rule of law and the rule of virtue? What's the difference from the old China ruled by an emperor centuries ago?"[4]

While repeated legislative motions, open letters, and protests against the system had yielded no results, in part due to resistance from the public-security and judicial bodies, outcry over Tang's case did have one immediate consequence: Tang was freed from the labor camp after just one week. She sued the labor camp and won, obtaining financial compensation (2,000 RMB) but failing to obtain a written apology: The court deemed that everyone had apologized sufficiently during the proceedings. Some Weibo users felt this was unacceptable. Wrote one: "Tang's victory is no cause for happiness. The government is willing to spend 10,000 RMB on 'stability maintenance,' but not to offer an apology to a suffering mother. The 2,000 RMB was more like charity than compensation."[5]

Stability maintenance, or *weiwen*, was another point of controversy in the case. Weibo users alleged that the government spent more money keeping Tang quiet and punishing her than compensating her or solving her case. The practice of stability maintenance involves the provision of central-government funds to local governments to ensure order, and Chinese media have alleged that the government spends more on stability maintenance than it does on national defense.

Exactly how stability is to be maintained is largely up to the local governments. In the past, such funds have been used to hire thugs to beat people or place troublesome protesters under unofficial house arrest. Money has been used to intimidate would-be protesters. All in all, the funds make possible a variety of extra-legal actions that often effectively "resolve" small incidents while sowing seeds of distrust and resentment among those affected.

The stability maintenance of Tang Hui was too much for some to tolerate. Not only was she denied justice for her victimized child, but she was punished for demanding it. Not only was she punished, but she was punished in an unjust way. Not only was she punished in an unjust way, but her unjust punishment neatly symbolized a hated system run by local and central governments.

The re-education-through-labor system was abolished after the Tang Hui debacle, albeit with some foot-dragging. State-run media announced that the system might be scrapped, but then removed the announcements from their websites. Later coverage emphasized that the program would be reformed. Finally, during the Third Plenum (an important meeting of the CCP Central Committee), officials announced that the re-education-through-labor system would be eliminated. By 2014, they seemed to have kept their word: Labor camps had been emptied of their prisoners, and converted to drug-rehabilitation centers or prisons.

Weibo is significant in the case of Tang Hui not because she was freed from the labor camp, but because the case both revealed and reaffirmed the higher expectations Chinese had for their judicial system and information transparency. Chinese internet users bonded over their investment in Tang's case and criticism of its handling. Weibo became a court of public opinion, and whether or not the online outcry was the causal factor in Tang's release, many Weibo users felt that their participation played a role in it.

Throughout Tang's journey, Weibo lowered barriers to entry for potential petitioners. Many users became virtual petitioners, directly contacting authorities involved in her case by leaving comments on posts written by authorities' official Weibo accounts. Whereas Tang Hui sacrificed money and time in her quest for justice, few Weibo users sacrificed more than a few hours or, at most, days. Yet the combined voices of those following the case on Weibo were perceived to have an impact. In this sense, Tang Hui's case was an exercise in public participation in debates about the law and justice system.

Weibo in some ways represents a somewhat more democratic alternative to China's traditional petitioning system. Instead of working from lower to higher authorities in the real world, any Weibo user can type up a complaint, upload pictures, and ask people to spread the word. In this collective experience, virtual onlookers serve as both amplifiers and witnesses to the petitioning process. A wronged individual can call attention to his or her grievances in a post without making a costly and potentially hazardous journey to Beijing.

For Tang, Weibo was a source of support when she reached the end of her rope. The publicity she drew, in part from the social-media platform, allowed her to challenge institutional wrongs and earn a modicum of individual justice. Private donors even made it possible for her to travel to the United States, to seek medical care for her daughter.

Her struggle was not without setbacks. In 2014 the courts decided to overturn the death sentences of two of the men who had raped her daughter, arguing that the circumstances surrounding the crime did not qualify as "especially serious." In a press conference, Tang expressed her dissatisfaction with the decision, but also her gratitude toward everyone who had struggled alongside her: "I thank all those journalists who helped me and internet users who championed my cause these past eight years," she said.[6]

Tang also responded to allegations of her own misconduct – that she should have watched her daughter more closely, that she had lied or exaggerated her claims to journalists, that she had acted irrationally while petitioning, that she had wasted public resources, or that she was simply stirring up a media frenzy for her own benefit. "Without intending to do so, I became a person of scrutiny in public debate," she said:

> I'm also a person with flaws, but I hope everyone can forgive me. I hope that in the future, the country's judicial system will be such that ordinary people like me do not have to sacrifice so much in order to achieve justice.[7]

The kebab vendor: Xia Junfeng

While Tang Hui's petitioning struck a chord with those Chinese upset with the public-security and judicial system, another man's experience became a rallying point for those who were upset with China's liberalizing economy and those it marginalized. In May of 2009, that man, Xia Junfeng, was selling kebabs along the street to make a living when urban enforcers, or *chengguan*, came by to check for permits. He didn't have a permit – most street vendors don't – and an altercation ensued. Xia claimed that after the two men began beating him, he stabbed them both to death in self-defense. As his case went to the courts, it also became the center of a national conversation about money, power, and justice.

Xia's case resonated with ordinary Chinese on many levels: economic inequality, judicial unfairness, and social injustice. Like Xia and his family, many people struggled to get by in China's rapidly liberalizing economy. Xia had once worked for a state-owned factory, but lost his job after market reforms allowed it to go bankrupt. Xia lived with his elderly parents, wife, and son, an only child. Xia and his wife, Zhang Jing, wanted to earn enough so that their son could study painting.

Many felt that the oppression of street vendors was unjust: Economic circumstances had forced the family to sell kebabs on the street to get by, but authorities would not even allow them to do that in peace. Even more unfairly, Xia did not receive due process at his trial. His defense lawyers were not allowed to submit some of their evidence or call witnesses from the scene. Most observers felt that the court's treatment of Xia demonstrated that not all were equal in the eyes of the law.

While Tang's case drew attention to the re-education-through-labor system, Xia's case drew attention to another despised institution: the *chengguan*, who are unique to China, and uniquely hated. They do the dirty work of the police, but receive none of the respect. In essence, they exist as a pseudo police force, established so that more legitimate law-enforcement agencies can outsource unpleasant tasks, like evicting residents from buildings marked for demolition or clearing out street vendors. There is little oversight, and numerous cases of *chengguan* brutality have made headlines over the past several years, further worsening their image.[8]

Prominent lawyer and rights activist Teng Biao defended Xia in his appeal by condemning the *chengguan* system, which carries out law-enforcement duties but has no clear legal juris-diction. He argued that executing Xia for defending himself would "embolden *chengguan*" by giving them the impression that they could beat citizens with impunity and "intimidate" those who would resist them.[9]

Ultimately, the courts sided against Xia in 2010 and sen-tenced him to death. His 2011 appeal was also rejected, and he was executed by lethal injection on September 25, 2013. There was widespread sympathy for Xia, and his name was the most searched term on Weibo the day of his execution. Many Weibo users shared posts made by his wife, detailing the call they had received and authorities' refusal of Xia's last request: He had wanted them to allow his family to take his picture, so his young son would have something to remember him by.

Sympathy also evolved into debate. At the time of his execution, many Weibo users had been following the case for years, through the trial, sentencing, appeal, and final decision. They argued about whether the playing field was level and the proceedings were just, and even whether Xia's legal team made errors in their public image campaign. Debate did not center on whether Xia killed the two men — he had — but on whether he received a fair trial, whether he deserved the harshest sentence possible, and how it could have been avoided.

Outside the courtroom, Xia's defense team carried out a public-relations campaign to raise funds for Xia's family as well as to pay his legal fees. To this end they exhibited and sold the artwork of Xia's son. Eventually, they compiled his paintings into a book available online for about $21; the initial printing of 50,000 sold out in just three months. These and other actions drew attention and support from many celebrities; the famous Taiwanese singer Annie Yi even adopted the boy as her own godson after Xia's execution.

But allegations that Xia's son, 13-year-old Xia Jianqiang, had plagiarized some of his paintings put a fly in the ointment. Jimmy Liao Fubin, the Taiwanese artist whom the younger Xia was accused of copying, declined to take legal action, but internet users had already begun to publish pictures of the younger Xia's paintings alongside those they closely resembled. Zhang Jing apologized, saying that her son had started imitating Liao's paintings years ago but would add his own twists to them. Still, the damage was done: Many who had been moved by the paintings depicting the family's struggles felt duped and betrayed.

The social-media spotlight was a double-edged sword for the Xia family. Though it helped raise necessary funds, it also led to increased scrutiny of their every move. But it may have been their only choice. Much as Xia felt backed into a corner by the *chengguan*, his family was also deprived of more preferable options, like a fair trial, or freedom to make a living in peace.

Public-relations campaigns had succeeded before in China, where courts had taken into account the sensitivity of an issue before rendering a verdict. Teng had reason to believe that this tactic might be successful: After all, in 2003, he had been part of a legal team that achieved policy-level reform in

China by publicizing the case of a single wronged individual named Sun Zhigang, an act that led to a decade of rights-defense-law activism. But this was not to be for Xia Junfeng: He died, and the *chengguan* system lived on.

Some changes did occur as a result of Xia's trial. Discussion about Xia's situation bolstered rising dissatisfaction with urban enforcers – not just at the individual level, but at the level of policy. Xia himself became a symbol of injustice, reinforcing rising dissatisfaction with China's judicial system. At the same time, sympathy for the *chengguan* he killed forced many to see the problem not as an isolated, individual conflict, but as a flaw in the system: a system that would continue to pit the economically disadvantaged against a hated, under-regulated pseudo police force. Weibo chatter brought into sharp relief the fact that Xia Junfeng's case was one that would be repeated until changes occurred in the system itself.

The watermelon vendor: Deng Zhengjia

Xia's case was not the first involving *chengguan* brutality, and it would not be the last. In 2013, *chengguan* attacked another street vendor, a man named Deng Zhengjia. Deng sold watermelons, not kebabs. He and his wife, Huang Xixi, grew the fruit near their home in rural Hunan province and sold them on the outskirts of a city about two hours' travel away by cart. It wasn't an easy life: They left at dawn, sold their fruit, and returned home, spending hours on the road and hours selling their fruit on the streets.

But on July 17, 2013, their hard life became much harder. *Chengguan* approached their cart and fined the couple 100 RMB, or about $15, for selling their wares without a license.

While they were issuing the fine, they also started to take some of the watermelons off the cart. Huang began to argue with the *chengguan*, demanding that they give the vendors written proof of the fine. When they did not, she called them bandits – and was summarily knocked unconscious. Huang told reporters that when she awoke, her husband was dead.

Eyewitnesses claimed that the *chengguan* had beaten Deng after knocking his wife unconscious. They told the *Beijing Times* that seven or eight *chengguan* had beaten Deng, who then lay on the ground, unmoving. Deng's sister-in-law, who said she was present when the incident occurred, told the paper that the *chengguan* had used the weights Deng brought for the melons as well as a steel pipe to beat him. She said that when the *chengguan* realized they had beaten him to death, they fled – but Deng's hand still clutched a lanyard holding one of their work identification cards, torn off during the fight. With this information and, by this point, dozens of eyewitnesses, Deng's family began to fight back.[10]

The city's emergency-management account on Weibo did not agree with the eyewitness accounts: They maintained that Deng had "suddenly collapsed and died." Thereafter, the post argued, the city and county Party committees and governments "took it very seriously" and "quickly ordered relevant departments" to get to the bottom of the incident. They stressed that the investigation was "ongoing."[11]

This post went viral on Weibo, largely because the idea that Deng had "suddenly collapsed and died" seemed like bullshit, even to people who had not been present on the scene. It was just one in a long series of equally implausible causes of death: In 2009, a man died after being arrested for cutting down trees without permission. The police said that he "died from playing hide-and-seek." According to the official explanation, he had gotten into an altercation with another inmate while playing the game and hit his head against the wall, suffering a cerebral hemorrhage. Others have famously died in police custody from "drinking boiled water," "slipping and falling," "having a nightmare," and "getting too excited."

Nobody believed those stories, and nobody believed that Deng had "suddenly collapsed and died." Deng's widow told a reporter for CCTV that her husband had been healthy, with no history of heart disease. "The government is avoiding responsibility," she claimed.[12]

The next day, things took a turn for the worse. Deng's relatives gathered around his body early that morning in the village where he lived, and a large group of police arrived on the scene. There was an altercation, after which several of Deng's family members were hospitalized. Police then dragged Deng's body away and left it on the road leading to his home town. An official claimed that the police were just trying to help the family members move the body, but one of those who had been beaten rejected the idea: "Why did so many people get injured if [the police] were just helping the family?" he asked. "Obviously, they were lying. What they wanted to do was to cremate the body and destroy the evidence."[13]

After the altercation, Deng's younger daughter logged in to her verified Weibo account and spoke out: "All the people in Linwu county who have been active in raising awareness of my father's case on Weibo and online forums have been asked to stop sharing and commenting," she wrote:

> The autopsy results indicate that my father suffered a hemorrhage in his brain. The government is trying to cover up the truth. My father has been said to have

had "a heart disease or other sudden disease." What the government is doing is totally unacceptable![14]

Weibo users reposted her message more than 100,000 times – propelling it to the top of the site's trending posts – but, later that day, it disappeared. Her words of protest were then replaced with a short statement: "The government has comforted my family in a proper way. We are content with what they have done."[15] This comment went viral as well, as many users speculated that the family had been threatened or bribed to keep quiet – or some combination of both. It later came to light that authorities had compensated Deng's family to the tune of almost $150,000. Locals told CCTV that for every day Deng's family delayed in accepting the deal, their compensation would be reduced.

Despite the success authorities had in resolving the claims of Deng's family, the anger over the incident did not dissipate. It became a national affair, one surrounding issues of economic justice, poor oversight for *chengguan*, and local-government corruption. Weibo users considered the implications that such a system might have for a society's future.

One response to the case of Deng Zhengjia resonated deeply with Weibo users: It was an essay by Li Chengpeng about Deng's life and death. In it, Li pled with businessmen not to remain silent about injustice in China, arguing that in an unpredictable system, their fate was just as unassured as Deng's. In the seizure of Deng's watermelons, he saw the unfair seizure of assets like land throughout China. He wrote that Deng had been living his own "Chinese dream," a dream cut short by *chengguan* brutality. "Before we sit down to talk about the Chinese dream," Li argued, "you should protect a watermelon vendor's dream."[16]

Li's essay was reposted almost 200,000 times, making it far and away the top post of the day and week. The essay caused such a stir that Li was reportedly barred from posting on Weibo for one month. And he was not the only one to stand up for Deng. Pseudonymous Weibo celebrity Zuoyeben followed the case and supported the family, defending them against critics after they accepted compensation from the government: "We cannot imagine how hard it is for a family in a rural area to stand up against their local government," he wrote on Weibo. "It would be a life worse than death."[17]

Authorities were able to resolve most of the tension surrounding Deng's death with money – and likely politically pressure – but they could not contain the damage done to the image of the local government so easily. In addition, since the debate surrounding the incident reached national proportions, more observers criticized the central government for their obviously deliberate inaction.

Chengguan brutality would have been a sensitive issue with or without Weibo – but Weibo effectively gathered all of the tinder for the uproar in one virtual space and connected theoretical discussions about local-government systems and economics to widespread dismay over one man's tragic death. When the *chengguan* beat Deng to death, it became even clearer that instances of individual injustice resonated with mainstream Chinese society – that there were no isolated incidents anymore.

The rights-defense movement and the New Citizens' Movement

Issues like these – land seizures, wrongful deaths, and miscarriages of justice – have often led individuals in China to see their problems as part of larger, systemic issues. Over the years, the number of people in China willing to speak out about these issues has grown, swelling into a small but vocal minority that champions the cause of rights defense. In spite of the risks and obstacles to their success, in a country where speaking truth to power has led to imprisonment and death in the recent past, they have pushed the boundaries of what is allowed to create more space for themselves and others to live, work, pray, and protest with dignity.

Perhaps one of the highest-profile activists to walk this path is Chen Guangcheng, a self-taught lawyer. Chen became famous in 1996, after he won a case against his local government. He argued that officials were collecting taxes from people with disabilities (like himself—Chen is blind), when by law these families were exempt. After Chen's success, he began to advise and defend others in his home town on legal matters. Over the course of his career he has worked on a broad range of issues, including pollution and illegal land seizures.

Chen may be best known for standing up for the women in his home town of Linyi, Shandong province, who were made to have late-term abortions or forcibly sterilized during the enforcement of China's one-child policy, which restricts most Chinese citizens to a single child. In 2005, he sued local family-planning officials over the rights violations. Chen sought to publicize the case, the first of its kind, by meeting with foreign media, and initially his efforts seemed successful. But later that year the local government retaliated by placing him under illegal house arrest, and, in 2006, he was charged with inciting others to violent protest, charges he has said are merely trumped-up. Local authorities turned back his lawyers, including prominent activist Xu Zhiyong, during court proceedings, and the court found Chen guilty after only two hours. He would spend the next four years in prison.

Even after his release, Chen remained under house arrest, constantly watched and restricted. But by 2010, many things had changed since his early days as an activist, not least among them the advent of social-media platforms like Weibo and Twitter. Word of Chen's activism and imprisonment had drawn supporters from around the world, many of whom networked with each other to provide support to Chen and his family.

During Chen's illegal detention, he became something of an internet phenomenon – others took pictures of themselves wearing sunglasses and posted them in solidarity. A political cartoonist who goes by the pen name Crazy Crab collected these pictures through an online campaign and posted them on a website established for the purpose. International organizations had lobbied China to release Chen, and activists throughout China rallied behind him.

And then, something truly amazing happened – Chen escaped, with the aid of fellow activists Guo Yushan and He Peirong. Both Guo and He used Twitter to support reform movements in China. News of Chen's escape spread like wildfire among fellow activists and supporters – though censorship on Weibo quickly kicked into gear. It was through Twitter that activists managed to publish Chen's initial statements out to a wider audience and translate them through crowdsourced efforts.

Chen eventually made it to the US embassy in Beijing, and from there he traveled with his family to the United States, where he spent a year in residence at New York University. Some of those who have stayed behind have been less fortunate: Guo Yushan, who helped him escape, was placed under house arrest, and his think tank, which advocated liberalization, was raided and banned in 2013. In 2014, he was detained by police and now faces charges of "provoking trouble."

Many lawyers who started out as rights defenders like Chen – working to protect clients wronged by their local governments or those whose freedom of speech had been restricted – gradually came to focus on even broader issues. At the root of local-government corruption, they saw a lack of transparency and judicial independence, which has allowed those in power to amass fortunes and sway the hand of justice.

Similarly, it was an individual incident that started several of China's most influential reformers of the twenty-first century down the path to national-level activism. The man at the center of that incident was named Sun Zhigang. In 2002, 27-year-old Sun had traveled from his home in the central city of Wuhan to the southern megalopolis of Guangzhou for work. He had graduated from university, where he studied fashion design, but left for Guangzhou because he had found a job there in a garments factory. Life seemed to be going fine for a few months.

But by March of the next year, something had gone wrong. Sun was detained by authorities in a holding center. By Chinese law, he should not have been working outside his home province without legal permission, yet such permission was difficult to obtain. After a short time in detention, Sun died in police custody. An autopsy revealed that he had been brutally beaten.

Sun's case began to attract attention throughout the country after his parents contacted journalists at the *Southern Metropolis Daily* in Guangdong. It was only 2003, and the internet was young in China, but news of Sun's death had gone viral – it was through the internet, specifically Peking

University's online forum, Yitahutu, that a young man named Xu Zhiyong learned of his death.

Rights movements everywhere use the internet to reach new audiences, but the web has always been especially popular among Chinese activists. Even in the early days of the Chinese internet, online protest played a pivotal role in coordinating activism. The internet was still tiny in 2003, but it connected many scholars and university students through university-based message boards. Xu, then a law doctoral student at Peking University, learned of the case through Yitahutu and then contacted his fellow students and friends Teng Biao and Yu Jiang. Through emails and telephone calls, they developed a recommendation for reform to China's custody and repatriation system and submitted it to the country's legislature. In August, the law establishing detention centers was repealed and online chatter died down.

Emboldened by this success, Xu, Teng, Yu, and others continued to speak out. But they saw first-hand the after-effects of successful protest: The *Southern Metropolis Daily*, which had gone all-in with its coverage of the Sun Zhigang case, was targeted by the government, and its general manager, Yu Huafeng, was charged with graft and bribery. Xu served as a defense lawyer for Yu, but they lost their case: Yu spent the next four years behind bars. Around that time, Xu's own "Sunshine Constitutionalism" website, which advocated social progress and rights defense, was blocked.

In the years following this initial backlash, Xu, Teng, and others pursued legal reform and rights defense. They formed another group, the Open Constitution Initiative (OCI). They protested the shutdown of Peking University's Yitahutu forum, and were kicked out of their office space. They continued to work together throughout the 2000s, researching issues, representing clients in cases of land disputes, recommending reform, and promoting the development of China's civil society.

By 2005, Xu had been beaten trying to visit Chen Guangcheng, and had run into any number of walls in his other efforts. But he persisted, running as an independent candidate for Beijing's municipal legislature. In 2006, he was elected to the People's Congress of the district in Beijing where he lived. The OCI helped to educate and train others interested in running as independent candidates, while they continued to take on sensitive legal cases. In 2008, he and others worked to win compensation for the children poisoned by melamine-tainted milk that had left more than 50,000 infants hospitalized and killed four.

Eventually, authorities cracked down on the group and charged the OCI with tax evasion in 2009. Through donations from their supporters, they were able to pay the fines, but authorities shut down the organization and stripped more than 50 lawyers of their license to practice. That year, Xu was detained by police for longer than a month.

When he was released, Xu and his followers continued to support the development of China's civil society. They launched another movement – the New Citizens' Movement – with a blog post entitled "China needs a new citizens' movement." The post was deleted but continues to circulate online. In it, Xu argued:

> There must be an end to tyranny, but the New Citizens' Movement is far from being just a democratic reformation; the New Citizens' Movement's discourse is not "overthrow," but "establish." It is not one social class taking the place of another social class, but letting

righteousness take its place in the Chinese nation. It
is not hostility and hate, but universal love.[18]

Xu's declaration signaled a new beginning and a new center of
gravity for the movement: Many of its members had worked
for years in the OCI or as rights-defense activists; quite a few
knew each other from work, school, or other activities. But
the New Citizens' Movement was founded online. In his essay,
Xu explicitly acknowledged the role of the web in the movement's growth, writing: "The internet, telecommunications,
and other new technologies have sped up China's enlighten-
ment and the formation of citizens' interpersonal networks."

In the years that followed, Xu and others frequently used
Weibo and Twitter to raise awareness of civil-rights issues.
In addition to sharing information, though, members of the
movement also organized offline activities, among them the
"same-city dinners," or "citizen banquets," that were discussed
in a previous chapter.

It has always been hard for members of this community
to work toward change and greater awareness while avoiding
harsh repercussions. Take the "same-city dinner gatherings,"
for example: some want to promote the activities broadly,
while others fear attracting too much attention. If no one
speaks about the activities with journalists, there is a chance
authorities might see them as less of a threat. Perhaps such
a course of action could not guarantee indefinite safety, this
line of thinking goes, but it might buy a little time for the
gatherings to catch on in more cities.

The fear of a crackdown is rooted in the reality that
many active members of the New Citizens' Movement frequently endure verbal harassment and even physical abuse
during the course of their work. They have been detained,

interrogated, and subjected to violence for visiting other individuals engaged in the same work. In many of these cases, they rely on Twitter and Weibo to keep others aware of their location and status.

Teng Biao, now a visiting scholar in Hong Kong, described one such incident to the *Wall Street Journal* in 2010. Security forces had dragged him and a friend to the police station for visiting the mother of a fellow activist. The officers beat him and threatened to bury him in a hole, but Teng said he felt a bit safer because, while the officers were calling for reinforcements, he had sent out a message on Twitter calling attention to his situation.[19]

This is not uncommon for Chinese activists. In these circumstances, the activists will notify their friends on Twitter and Weibo, who activate virtual phone trees. When they can get the badge numbers of the police in question, or the phone numbers of the stations where they are being held, their friends and followers will make it known to the security forces that no one is going to turn a blind eye to abuse. This is called "requesting attention" or *qiu guanzhu* – when someone posts on Weibo or Twitter about an urgent situation with the police, they ask for attention, and their followers then retweet the original post. By circulating the information, they raise awareness and can often mobilize people in the area to check in on the activists.

The internet has helped in individual cases, but 2014 saw setback after setback for the New Citizens' Movement. Since Xi Jinping began to solidify his control, democracy advocates, rights protectors, and champions of reform have fallen quietly, individually, in low-profile cases here and there. Perhaps more cautious because of the power of the internet to draw attention to protests, authorities have chosen to divide and conquer. This is true with the government's strategy to put down the New Citizens' Movement. First, it shut down all related organizations, either by kicking members out of their offices or shutting down their businesses. Then, it charged them with tax violations. Finally, it began to systematically go after the movement's participants, arresting more than 40 in total by the end of 2013. Arrests continued throughout 2014. By the end of the year, many of the movement's most prominent members were behind bars, or living outside mainland China.

Some of those detained, sentenced, and jailed were convicted for only the smallest of protests. This was certainly true of the "Xinyu Three": Li Sihua, Liu Ping, and Wei Zhongping, all residents of Xinyu county in Jiangxi province. In April 2013, they held up signs calling for officials to declare their assets and for Xi Jinping to end dictatorship, and then posted the images online. This simple act drew a severe backlash. Authorities arrested them for "inciting subversion of state power" just six days later. By mid-2014, they had all been sentenced to prison, their sentences ranging from three to six and a half years.

Liu Ping was once a steel-factory worker. She lived an ordinary life until she was laid off in 2009 and lived off a very low fixed income. She fought back, for herself and her former co-workers, and was able to obtain some compensation. Following that, she and two other Xinyu locals, Wei Zhongping and Li Sihua, tried to run as independent candidates for a local legislature, and said that officials prevented them from being elected. Finally, they took up signs to protest an issue near to the hearts of many Chinese, especially those of lower socio-economic status: a lack of transparency surrounding government officials' wealth.

Wei, Liu, and Li were held for months before their October trial, far longer than is allowed by Chinese law. They were tortured while in detention, their defense lawyers said, and not officially charged until July, two months after their arrest. Their lawyers argued that their arrests and detention were part of a coordinated effort to take down the New Citizens' Movement. But Liu was not intimidated: "I have put into action all that I believe in," she said in her closing statement. "History will declare my innocence!"[20]

A court in Beijing had found two other members of the New Citizens' Movement guilty in January 2014, for similarly small-scale protests. Hou Xin and Yuan Dong were both convicted of "assembling a crowd to disturb public order" because they had held up a banner in Beijing in March 2013, calling for officials to disclose their assets. The courts allowed Hou to go free, but sentenced Yuan to a year and a half in prison. Lawyers for the two kept observers updated about the proceedings and sentencing via microblogging sites.

While Hou and Yuan received relatively light sentences, others did not. Authorities blamed activists Ding Jiaxi and Li Wei for inciting Hou and Yuan. Arrested on April 11, 2013, Ding and Li were labeled "ringleaders" and indicted in December of that year for "colluding with others to gather crowds to disrupt the order of public places" as well as "defying and obstructing the efforts of the state's public-safety-management personnel." Although they had not so much as held up a banner in a public place, Ding and Li were sentenced to three and a half and two years in prison respectively. Ding, who was a lawyer for many years and managed a firm for a decade, explained how many activists felt about the crackdown that had begun against the New Citizens' Movement: "Theoretically speaking, first-hand experience of prison time is an inevitable component of the citizens movement; it is only a matter of who experiences this," he wrote in a letter from prison. "Did we foresee it? We did foresee this day, except that it came much sooner than we thought."[21]

Authorities came for participants at all levels of the movement, but it was Xu Zhiyong whom they blamed for masterminding it. In April 2013, when many other movement members were taken by security forces, Xu Zhiyong was placed under house arrest. Around the same time, entrepreneur Wang Gongquan, a billionaire and activist for equal education rights for China's migrant population who had funded many of the movement's activities, was also arrested. Wang was released without charge, after months of interrogation, and authorities used some of his testimony in Xu's trial.

Xu was not formally arrested until July, and was charged with "gathering people to disturb public order" in December. On January 26, 2014, an intermediate court in Beijing found him guilty of "disturbing public order" and sentenced him to four years in prison. During the trial, the court had refused to allow the defense to call any of their 68 witnesses. The proceedings were closed to journalists and diplomats. In his concluding statement – of which he was only allowed to read part – Xu wrote to the courts and authorities who had jailed him: "By trying to suppress the New Citizens' Movement, you are obstructing China on its path to becoming a constitutional democracy through peaceful change."[22]

Even as the government has attempted to obstruct the New Citizens' Movement, or any movement that it considers a threat, activists have not given up. Even when they have repeatedly run into brick walls, petitioners like Tang Hui and activists like Liu Ping have affirmed that their struggles have meaning, despite resulting in great personal suffering. Their suffering, in turn, has inspired others to wonder what kind of a system would treat ordinary people so badly.

In the age of Weibo and other social media, their stories have become part of larger debates about justice, one in which people from all walks of life are passing judgment on the powerful – and, in many cases, demanding that they change.

six

THE CRACKDOWN AND THE CHINESE DREAM

The crackdown on the politically active minority described in the last chapter seemed to have little to do with the vast majority of Weibo users, but the rights-defense and New Citizens' Movement members were canaries in the coal mine of Chinese cyberspace. As authorities went after Xu Zhiyong and others, they pursued ordinary social-media users. A space apart from the closely monitored "real world," Weibo seemed a breath of fresh air to many, even those who weren't very politically minded. But real-name registration and censorship were only two aspects of an encroachment that eventually rendered the platform a shadow of its former self. In the late summer of 2013, authorities began targeting influential Weibo users as well as grass-roots activists. Through a series of punitive measures, they discouraged the use of Weibo to organize and challenge the official Party line.

During the early days of the crackdown, law enforcement detained hundreds of internet users across the country for offending Weibo messages and blog posts.[1] This was made easier by the announcement of a new judicial interpretation on September 6, 2013. According to this interpretation, which took effect on September 10, internet users who spread rumors on Weibo could face harsh punishment, as much as three years in jail, if their offending posts were shared more than 500 times or viewed more than 5,000 times. Those convicted of "spreading harmful rumors" could also face more serious punishment if they had been convicted of spreading rumors within the previous two years.

In addition, the interpretation broadened the definition of illegal content that "seriously harm[s] public order and national interests" – which could result in more serious punishment – to include online rumors that:

1. inspire collective action;
2. disrupt public order;
3. lead to ethnic or religious conflict;
4. are about multiple people and have a harmful societal impact;
5. harm China's image or seriously harm national interests;
6. create a negative international impact;
7. in any other way seriously harm public order and national interests.[2]

This new interpretation of China's criminal law was vague enough to threaten any social-media user whose online expression was deemed unacceptable by authorities. It gave rise to yet another internet-native neologism: "to be 500'ed." "Be careful, or you'll be 500'ed," Weibo users warned each other when commenting on posts containing potentially sensitive information. It did not escape the notice of many that the government was capable of ensuring any post it wished reached 500 reposts, thus putting its author in jeopardy.

The 2013 push was not the first so-called rumor crackdown. In 2011, a similar campaign was undertaken, shortly after the deadly Wenzhou train crash.[3] Another push occurred in 2012. But the 2013 crackdown had the most significant impact on Weibo.[4] In a January 2014 report released by the

China Internet Network Information Center (CNNIC), Weibo lost 27.8 million users in 2013, down 9.2 percent from a year before.[5] One London-based firm reported that Weibo activity declined by 40 percent in the last quarter of 2013.[6] Research conducted by East China Normal University's Institute for Data Science and Engineering, commissioned by the British *Telegraph* newspaper, showed even more clearly that Weibo use had plummeted 70 percent to a two-year low in the wake of the rumor crackdown.[7]

Silence in the flood: triumphs of censorship in a post-crackdown China

Weibo, the platform that was so closely tied to disaster relief in previous years did not remain so following the crackdown. In October 2013, Typhoon Fitow hit the coastal Chinese town of Yuyao, submerging 70 percent of its downtown area. Though tens of thousands were displaced and some residents went days without assistance, Weibo response was muted. During the Ya'an earthquake, users posted more than 7 million comments related to the disaster; during the flooding of Yuyao, the figure was around 170,000, according to official estimates.[8]

That's not to say there was nothing to talk about. Local residents clashed with police protecting a state-media crew, who had drawn ire by claiming that the worst of the flooding had passed.[9] Echoing past complaints, many Chinese wondered why riot suppression was so quick and effective while disaster relief was slow and uneven. Other users reposted a picture of an old man carrying a government official on his back so that the official's shoes did not get wet, leading Weibo users to condemn the selfishness of the bureaucrat's actions.

But no rage, sympathy, or mockery could gain much traction on Weibo. Among the most silent were online opinion leaders, celebrities, and public figures with millions of followers. These prominent users had lent their voices to causes like disaster relief in the past, but government efforts to rein in their influence led many to self-censor. In a post that was later deleted, one editor of a news magazine noted that neither sanctioned, traditional media nor grass-roots citizen journalists were covering the disaster comprehensively.[10]

One Weibo account run by the *Southern Metropolis Daily* offered its own explanation for the silence: "During the recent flooding of Yuyao, as the people emptied the shelves in supermarkets, the local government was busy detaining rumormongers." Since the government had begun a crackdown on online rumors, residents of the town and media reporting on site had perhaps decided that it would be better to live free, without comprehensive coverage of the typhoon's aftermath, than be jailed for a post made online.[11]

Entertaining ourselves to death

In the not-so-distant past, top posts on Weibo regularly garnered more than 100,000 reposts; but by the end of 2013, the top posts might have only 30 or 40,000. Before the crackdown, Weibo had plenty of posts about current events and scandals; after it, much of the content was skewed toward the commercial, with advertisements, funny gifs, and celebrity selfies dominating the lists of trending posts.

Part of this transformation is attributable to the targeting of influential users – known as "Big Vs" in China for the V present next to the online handles of verified users – who helped spread information by posting and reposting on important issues. These well-known users wielded outsized influence in the social-media sphere, where they championed any number of controversial causes, and that was precisely what authorities disliked. When they decided to rein in social media, they moved on Big Vs in a big way.

Sometime around the start of it all, China's national television network, CCTV, held a big public forum on the social responsibility of influential microbloggers and invited 14 of Weibo's more influential users to discuss the social-media platform's uses and impact. Among the guests were Pan Shiyi, a real-estate tycoon and one of Weibo's most prominent users, as well as Charles Xue, an angel investor and activist with more than 11 million Weibo followers, along with several posters who were either themselves government officials or were aligned with the government and Party.

Even in this fairly controlled setting, a talk in TV studios which was broadcast a week later on the program *Dialogue*, there was some debate. Pan Shiyi argued that influential Weibo users represented only themselves, while other guests defended the position that the more influential a Weibo user, the more he or she represented his or her organization or followers. Some of the guests said that rumors resulted from the lack of a verification system on Weibo, but one guest in particular disagreed: "The reason there are so many rumors," Charles Xue said in the program's opening trailer, "is because credibility has fallen." He went on to argue that controlling online speech would not resolve the problem of low credibility in government and society.

Ostensibly, the televised forum was an open discussion, but in reality it was a clear statement of the government's intention to come down hard on Weibo. Most of the invited guests spoke of the need for order, stability, and "positive energy." The host and audience members supported these views. During the forum, participants were encouraged to spread "positive energy" and avoid spreading rumors. Each time Pan or Xue would voice an opinion counter to the Party line – that influential microbloggers should stick to positive guidance and avoid negative speech – their speech would be followed by a comment from a more government-friendly voice, who would then receive applause from the audience or affirmation from the host. In essence, Pan's and Xue's arguments were showcased as examples of what not to do. The program also downplayed the role Weibo had played in unearthing the truth by circulating rumors later proven true.

Among the discussed topics was the use of Weibo to question and criticize. In particular, CCTV highlighted rumors that had circulated on Weibo that vast donations from large companies made after the Ya'an earthquake had failed to reach disaster victims. The topic led to a discussion on how responsible influential users were for ensuring the accuracy of the information they reposted, with guests differing in opinion. A number of the guests criticized Pan Shiyi for questionable messages he had reposted in his two years on Weibo; Pan defended himself by saying that he always apologized and corrected these posts when they were proven false.

The program also contained several other clues to punitive measures that would follow. At one point, the camera focused on an image of Taiwanese venture capitalist and avid Weibo user Kai-Fu Lee's Weibo page, implying he was an irresponsible Big V.[12] But Lee, who had more than 50 million followers on Weibo, was not present for the forum: Around the time the rumor crackdown began in earnest, he had moved to Taiwan to undergo treatment for cancer and greatly reduced his time spent on social media.

After the forum aired, authorities went on the offensive. First, they arrested two "rumormongers," Qin Zhihui (online handle Qin Huohuo) and Yang Xiuyu (online handle Li'erchaisi) on August 19. Authorities charged Qin and others with spreading a number of extremely sensational rumors; on August 21, the *Beijing Times* even ran an exposé on their company, which allegedly manipulated sentiment on Weibo for the highest bidder.[13] Instead of acknowledging that rumors were a symptom of a problem within the system, China's government labeled those whose "rumors" were deemed a threat to stability "rumormongers" and promoted the idea that rumormongers were soulless profiteers making money out of social instability.

Following the arrests of Qin and Yang came a more high-profile bust: Police arrested Charles Xue, the angel investor and outspoken critic with 11 million Weibo followers who had appeared on the CCTV program not so long before. Charles, an American citizen originally from China, was first detained on August 23 on charges of soliciting prostitutes. The lengthy airtime CCTV and other state-run media devoted to this during the network's flagship news program, unusual for an arrest of that nature, sent a signal to other prominent Weibo users that they might be next.

Authorities made the purpose of Xue's arrest even more explicit when CCTV later broadcast a segment on Xue entitled "The online journey of 'Big V' Xue Manzi," even referring to him by his online handle, not his legal name. The September 15 news program emphasized that Xue enjoyed "all kinds of honors" associated with internet celebrity, but "abandoned the responsibilities of an internet Big V," then showed footage of Xue himself emphasizing the need for rules to protect "order" online. The segment ended with clips of Xue in handcuffs, and behind bars, as the narrator announced that an investigation against Xue for his activities online was underway.[14]

Xue was once known for his activism: On Weibo, he drew attention to the plight of Tang Hui after she was sent to a re-education-through-labor camp.[15] He also was active in reposting information about the trafficking of children in China, a problem that Weibo had been influential in addressing. Yet he had fallen afoul of authorities for his cantankerous posts, often critical of the government's lack of transparency and accountability.

The character assassination of Xue complete, CCTV and other Party-line news outlets expanded their targets to the broader concept of "online rumors." Kai-Fu Lee, who often promoted free speech and rule of law, also came under fire. Where before, cinematography had merely implied his guilt, an op-ed in *Party Building*, a Communist magazine, came out attacking his character and even questioning whether he actually had cancer.[16]

Backlash within the system

The series of actions taken against public intellectuals began to split opinion within state-aligned news outlets. In August of 2013, a well-known CCTV producer named Wang Qinglei posted on Weibo about the network's recent activities: "The past two weeks have been disgraceful for our CCTV workers," he wrote. "Standards for news have been raped repeatedly by those in power: We avoided legal principles, setting in motion machines to promote a crackdown on internet rumors." Wang then complained that CCTV's treatment of Kai-Fu Lee and Charles Xue had been unethical, concluding: "The integrity and professionalism in the news has vanished totally and completely."[17]

Wang claimed that when CCTV fired him on November 27, they told him it was because of his Weibo posts questioning the network's treatment of the campaign against spreading rumors. In a lengthy open letter Wang wrote upon leaving CCTV, his employer for ten years, he speculated that the network's motivation for firing him was to "kill one to warn a hundred." Although there were "many people at CCTV" with mindsets like his own, he argued, he was targeted because he spoke what they were all thinking.[18] Wang's letter was deleted shortly after its posting to Weibo, but other users who had seen and saved the file continued to re-upload it to the site, where it got tens of thousands of reposts. Almost everyone who was paying attention on Weibo in November had either read the letter or heard about why Wang left CCTV. What began as a war on rumors had casualties far beyond the kind of libel that such a campaign would ostensibly target.

There is an argument for laws against spreading rumors: In many countries, it can be considered libel, at least, and if it doesn't result in jail time, it may still end in fines or other forms of punishment. Yet aspects of China's legal system make the law a dangerous tool, one that can be used to suppress opposition to an unjust system. A September 15 Caixin Online editorial entitled "Rumors and the power of deception" hit at the crux of the issue, citing rumors surrounding the corruption case of an official named Liu Tienan, who once headed the National Energy Administration (NEA) and served on the powerful National Development and Reform Commission (NDRC). Before Liu was sacked, the NEA threatened to prosecute anyone who spread rumors about Liu's alleged corruption. Yet eventually it became clear that Liu himself was to be prosecuted, and the NEA made no move to take back its earlier threats: "If we look at the whole country, similar cases are not rare," concluded Caixin Online columnist Xin Haiguang. "It appears government officials have the right to lie and the public has become inured to such practices."[19]

The public may have come to expect such treatment, but that does not mean they are happy with it. Of course there are a few who have applauded the increased restrictions on free speech, but they were already true believers – little could happen that would change their minds about the Party. For the rest, at best, it has gone under the radar. People who don't post on Weibo or read the news probably care little about journalists who have been arrested or celebrities forced to confess to crimes on television. But for those who do care – those who are most likely to believe in the power of their voices and China's political progress – these incidents are poisonous. For them, China's war on rumors has stoked resentment against arbitrary punishments, hollow political slogans, paternalistic government measures, and hypocrisy.

The Chinese dream

Perhaps in part to soften the blows, China's leadership – and Xi Jinping in particular – offered a carrot to the crackdown's stick: the "Chinese dream." The idea, thought to be Xi's own effort to promote nationalist sentiment and unity, offered a vision of the future to replace all the others it had deleted in the heavy-handed "cleansing" of online spaces and public protests. Chinese-dream-related rhetoric began churning out in full force in the spring of 2013, shortly after Xi became president on March 14.

The Chinese dream was an all-fronts, no-holds-barred propaganda campaign that promoted, in Xi's own words, "the great renewal of the Chinese nation." Unlike the American dream, which basically entails individual financial success and home ownership, the Chinese dream is one of collective sacrifice for the common good. In a letter to a group of students, Xi emphasized that "only by integrating individual dreams to the national cause can one finally make great achievement."[20]

This feel-good campaign (accompanied by songs, television shows, and essay contests) was a precursor to the later, more punitive tactics used to achieve unity. In June of 2013, Xi announced to top officials the beginning of a "self-purification" campaign intended to eliminate "formalism, bureaucracy, hedonism, and extravagance" among China's government workers. State media later took to calling this a "mass-line" campaign, referencing Mao Zedong's movement to promote ideological conformity.[21] Xi Jinping's campaigns echoed other Maoist techniques. Top leaders stressed the importance of "criticisms and self-criticisms" – another Maoist throwback – and warned against Western values and democracy.[22]

Campaigns that followed this were even more ideologically focused. In August, the push for ideological unity expanded from cadres to common citizens.[23] Propaganda authorities announced mandatory classes on Marx for all Chinese journalists.[24] Party-line media ramped up on exhortations to journalists to focus on "positive" coverage in support of the Party's aims. And of course, authorities kicked off an all-out war on "online rumors."

Yet the Chinese-dream campaign had an unexpected side effect: The term became a touchstone for criticism of the CCP. When reports surfaced of children too poor to buy shoes, netizens asked: "Is this their Chinese dream?" In the comments sections of articles about the rising cost of living, worsening job market for college graduates, and preventable disasters, critics asked: "How does the government expect us to realize the 'Chinese dream' when we can't even fix these basic problems?"

Weibo was one of the main spaces in which the Chinese-dream rhetoric encountered pushback. Chinese using Weibo saw the unending talk about the Chinese dream as a spring-board to discuss the government's failures and responsibilities. Many offered their own definitions of the Chinese dream. In late March, petitioners gathered in Beijing co-opted the term to protest injustices they'd suffered. They held up signs that offered their own definitions of the Chinese dream; some said it was the government returning land that had been taken from them, others said it was judicial fairness.[25]

In years past, journalists and scholars discussed a "Chinese dream," but interpretations varied. It was more a rhetorical tool than a properly thought-out idea. But the Party's decision to promote a well-defined "Chinese dream" was tantamount to a declaration that the CCP knows best. The official anointing of a Chinese dream, singular, signaled the resolve of China's new administration to lead by designating a correct path.

The effort to promote the Chinese dream backfired as most people expressed criticism of the term, or at least became fatigued by it. The money poured into promoting the seemingly meaningless campaign became a farce, drawing attention to all of the problems from which it seemed to be a diversion. In short, efforts to shove a one-size-fits-all set of aspirations down the throats of more than 1.3 billion people with different backgrounds, value systems, and worldviews has fallen short of total success. And that's a good thing – the dissent, divergence, and diversity that thrive despite any manner of authoritarian measures are what will carry China into the future.

No more Mr. Nice Guy: from public-opinion guidance to the public-opinion "struggle"

Sadly, continued resistance to this imposed national narrative has not moved Chinese authorities to soften their strategy. Instead, they've decided they weren't being tough enough. In late August 2013, state- and Party-run media began to emphasize the importance of "winning the public-opinion struggle" – both through positive propaganda like that about the Chinese dream and elimination of more negative factors. The term was troubling, and not just because it was a throw-back to the chaotic Cultural Revolution. If there is a struggle to be won, then logically some online voices are "enemies" to be struggled against. In September, official rhetoric became even more heated: Opinion pieces spoke of "baring blades" and a "fight to the death." Even though such language was figurative, it signaled that consequences for internet critics could become much worse.[26]

Since the arrival of the internet in China, authorities have sought to use it and control it. In the past, these measures were called "public-opinion guidance" – the use of censor-ship as well as propaganda to steer an easily misled public in the right ideological direction. Yet in 2013, authorities transitioned from guidance to battle, signaling a shift from a softer paternalism to a more disciplinary stance.

Let 100 flowers bloom

Allowing discussion to flourish before cracking down on those deemed too critical or too dangerous is a People's Republic tradition. In the early years of the PRC, Mao Zedong had gained almost total control, and had strict standards for ideological conformity. But, in 1957, he pushed forward a campaign of free expression that had begun to take shape the year before. This movement was called the "100 Flowers Campaign," based on the expression, "Let 100 flowers bloom, let 100 schools of thought contend." The idea behind it was that China's intellectuals could come up with ways to improve the existing system and take part in shaping their country's future.

In February 1957, Mao gave the speech entitled "On the correct handling of contradictions among the people," in which he famously stated:

> All attempts to use administrative orders or coercive measures to settle ideological questions or questions of right and wrong are not only ineffective but harmful [...] The only way to settle questions of an ideological nature or controversial issues among the people is by the democratic method, the method of discussion, criticism, persuasion, and education, and not by the method of coercion or repression.[27]

In the beginning, criticism was freely allowed, and a number of prominent intellectuals came out with ideas that would have been grounds for imprisonment, if not worse, just months before. From May to June of that year, critics sent millions of letters with a variety of suggestions to the premier's office. They held protests and meetings, published scathing articles, and erected a democracy wall – a public bulletin board on which anyone could place critical posters, letters, or poems calling for change.

On July 7, Mao ended the campaign, and shortly thereafter began what became known as the Anti-Rightist Movement, a harsh crackdown on the same intellectuals who had responded to the call for free expression. The Anti-Rightist Movement lasted for about two years, during which hundreds of thousands were persecuted. Some were simply criticized, others were forced to undergo "re-education through labor." Still others were executed. Even the law came under attack: Authorities transferred legal professionals to other work units and their jobs were taken over by police and political officials.

It had seemed, at first, that Mao's support of the 100 Flowers Campaign was a vote of confidence in the socialist system – that he was confident it could compete in a free market of ideas with all other possibilities and come out the winner. Once the crackdown began, many suspected that Mao had never been serious about opening China's government, much less himself, up to constructive criticism. Many believed instead that he had planned the ensuing crackdown from the beginning, and had supported the 100 Flowers Campaign in order to root out those who were ideologically opposed to himself.

In the years since the 100 Flowers Campaign, leaders have used this tactic again and again. In 1978, just after the Cultural Revolution, Deng Xiaoping and others allowed activists to erect another democracy wall, this time in the center of Beijing. People converged on a wall in the central part of the city, posting criticisms of the government and poetry. But this period, known as the Beijing Spring, was short-lived. In 1979, authorities moved the wall to a new location. Then they restricted access, requiring visitors to show identification. Then, they shut it down amid a crackdown on political dissent, jailing one of the Democracy Wall critics for over a decade.

Many see the past repeating itself in China's online spaces. With Weibo – which some have called a modern-day democracy wall – constrained discussion of sensitive issues was allowed, and even encouraged. Authorities took into account public outcry in judicial decisions and policy. Then they began requiring visitors to show identification. Then they ramped up the targeting – and jailing – of individual users.

But allowing Weibo to have a two-year heyday gave authorities information they desperately needed. That's one aspect of Chinese social media that is often overlooked: its function as a mechanism for delivering feedback to the government. It is clear from publicly available information that China has invested heavily in learning from social media. Chinese authorities have admitted that there are 2 million people in the country working as "online public-opinion analysts," professional web surfers who sift through social-media content and write reports on their findings.[28] And much more has undoubtedly been spent behind the scenes to learn what people are really saying online. After all, in order to win the "public-opinion struggle," as the CCP has pledged it will do, it must first understand public opinion.

But when it became clear that the pot might boil over, authorities tightened restrictions on Weibo and punished those thought to be the most outspoken. They made examples out of intellectuals who voiced dissenting views and protested for change. One Chinese historian, Zhang Lifan, even called the crackdown an "Internet anti-rightist campaign."[29] Most importantly, authorities allowed vocal protesters to voice their opinions, and then punished them months, even years later, which further warned would-be activists that the state might come for them when they least expected it.

This practice of waiting until the time is right to exact revenge is known in Chinese as "settling accounts after the autumn." In ancient times, rulers would execute criminals just before winter. Spring was a season of new beginnings, and in the summer people were busy in the fields. In the fall and winter, however, they were idler. Local officials had an easier time assembling villagers to watch executions then, so the acts were more intimidating, and the warnings likely served to curb crime in a season when people had more time to break the law.

In modern times, Chinese authorities have often employed the practice as a form of crisis management. When there has been a protest or petitioners, they appease those demanding change or justice by promising to punish offenders, right wrongs, and return money or land. Once observers have moved on or tired of the story, they pursue and punish those thought to have coordinated the protests or petitions, making their lives difficult in any number of ways and setting an example for others who would follow in their footsteps.

There is cause for worry in these parallels, but there is also hope: Many of the intellectuals who were purged during the Anti-Rightist Movement and later movements were released, rehabilitated, and regained power in the aftermath of these ideologically restrictive periods. Once it became clear in the 1970s that China needed to recover from the chaos and economic stagnation of the Cultural Revolution, Deng Xiaoping, once a political outcast, was able to gain enough political support to push unprecedented economic reforms and retained significant amounts of power, even after his retirement in 1990.

Purged twice during the Cultural Revolution, Deng was forced out of his high-level positions for holding ideological and economic views at odds with Mao. Red Guards harassed his family and tortured his son, who later jumped out of a four-story window in a suicide attempt that left him a paraplegic. Deng later returned as one of the most powerful leaders China had ever known.

The point of this lengthy historical tangent is that history has a way of surprising us – that the things we feel are so solid and permanent may transform completely, often while we are paying attention to other things. Historical tragedies, like the Anti-Rightist Movement, will repeat themselves – but so will triumphs, pushes for reform, brave acts of resistance, and the everyday work that adds up to a better future.

By sharing their hopes and fears with each other, China's social-media users have been part of that work. They have made it clear that the Chinese dream is not a singular aim for national glory, but the sum of as many different dreams as there are people in the world's largest country. Whether the rich and powerful acknowledge this to be true, it is the lived reality for China's city dwellers and farmers, rich and poor, protesters and apolitical. Social media has nurtured their belief in their right to dream, a belief that has been growing stronger amid China's political and economic development. Expectations of transparency, accountability, and justice, being formless, are not easily contained.

The number of Chinese who use the internet is only going to increase in the coming years, and their ability to use it for their own purposes will only grow more sophisticated, perhaps in ways that the government will like and certainly in ways that it will not. When China's government officials realize they cannot change this, they will be forced to change themselves.

Notes

Introduction

1 "China: internet usage stats and population report," Internet World Stats: Usage and Population Statistics (website). Available at http://www.internetworldstats.com/asia/cn.htm (accessed March 1, 2015).

2 《中国互联网络发展状况统计报告》，中国互联网络信息中心，2014年7月。["34th statistical report on internet development in China," China Internet Network Information Center (website), July 2014.] Available at http://www.cnnic.cn/hlwfzyj/hlwxzbg/hlwtjbg/201407/P020140721507223212132.pdf (accessed March 1, 2015).

3 "32nd statistical report on internet development in China," China Internet Network Information Center (website), July 2013. Available at http://www1.cnnic.cn/IDR/ReportDownloads/201310/P020131029430558704972.pdf (accessed March 1, 2015). Maeve Duggan and Joanna Brenner, "The demographics of social media users – 2012," Pew Research Center (website), February 14, 2013. Available at http://pewinternet.org/Reports/2013/Social-media-users/The-State-of-Social-Media-Users.aspx (accessed March 1, 2015).

4 Jon Sullivan, "China's Weibo: is faster different?," *New Media & Society* xvi/1 (February 2013), pp. 24–37. Available at http://nms.sagepub.com/content/16/1/24 (accessed March 1, 2015).

1. Cover-ups and Uncoverings

1 S. Hernandez, "Directives from the ministry of truth: Wenzhou high-speed train crash," *China Digital Times*, July 25, 2011. Available at http://chinadigitaltimes.net/2011/07/directives-from-the-ministry-of-truth-wenzhou-high-speed-train-crash/ (accessed March 1, 2015).

2 "温州动车追尾舆情解读：动车之殇 微博中的民意涌动"《人民网》2011年7月28日。["An analysis of public opinion about the Wenzhou train crash: a train tragedy and an outpouring of public sentiment on Weibo," *People's Daily Online*, July 28, 2011.] Available at https://web.archive.org/web/20121229163606/http://society.people.com.cn/GB/223265/15272664.html (accessed March 1, 2015).

3 Sharon LaFraniere and Michael Wines, "In baring facts of train crash, blogs erode China censorship," *New York Times*, July 28, 2011.

Available at http://www.nytimes.com/2011/07/29/world/asia/29china.html?pagewanted=all&_r=0 (accessed March 1, 2015).

4 Charlie Custer, "The Wenzhou crash and the future of Weibo," Tech in Asia (website), August 1, 2011. Available at http://www.techinasia.com/the-wenzhou-crash-and-the-future-of-weibo/ (accessed March 1, 2015).

5 Sophie Beach, "Poll: 98% say Wenzhou train buried to destroy evidence," *China Digital Times*, July 25, 2011. Available at http://chinadigitaltimes.net/2011/07/poll-98-say-wenzhou-train-buried-to-destroy-evidence/ (accessed March 1, 2015).

6 Adam Minter, "Train crash proves debacle for China's propaganda machine," Bloomberg (news agency), July 28, 2011. Available at http://www.bloomberg.com/news/2011-07-29/train-crash-proves-debacle-for-china-s-propaganda-machine-adam-minter.html (accessed March 1, 2015).

7 Anthony Ellwood-Russell, "Wenzhou train crash one year memorial," Danwei (website), July 29, 2012. Available at http://www.danwei.com/wenzhou-train-crash-one-year-memorial/ (accessed March 1, 2015).

8 《2013年铁道统计公报》，国家铁路局，2014年4月。["2013 rail statistics public report," National Railway Administration of the People's Republic of China (website), April 2014.] Available at http://www.nra.gov.cn/fwyd/zlzx/hytj/201404/t20140410_5830.htm (accessed March 1, 2015).

9 The most popular Weibo platform is Weibo.com, the web address of Sina Weibo, a platform where users can create, share, and comment on short blog posts. Tencent and Sohu, two other internet companies, have their own Weibo platforms, but "Weibo" generally refers to Sina Weibo, unless otherwise specified.

10 "China: more than 4.8 million homeless in Sichuan quake: official," ReliefWeb (website), May 16, 2008. Available at http://reliefweb.int/report/china/china-more-48-million-homeless-sichuan-quake-official (accessed March 1, 2015).

11 "Freight train derails in Gansu after quake; explosion feared," China.org.cn, May 13, 2008. Available at http://www.china.org.cn/china/local/2008-05/13/content_15195285.htm (accessed March 1, 2015).

12 Peter Ford, "China sentences quake activist Tan Zuoren," *Christian Science Monitor*, February 9, 2010. Available at http://www.csmonitor.com/World/Asia-Pacific/2010/0209/China-sentences-quake-activist-Tan-Zuoren (accessed March 1, 2015). "Chinese earthquake activist Tan Zuoren released after five-year prison term," *Guardian*, March 27, 2014. Available at http://www.theguardian.com/world/2014/mar/27/chinese-activist-tan-zouren-released-five-year-prison-term (accessed March 1, 2015).

13 Silke Wünsch, "China's Li Chengpeng wins top honors at The Bobs online activism award," Deutsche Welle (website), May 7, 2013. Available at http://www.dw.de/chinas-li-chengpeng-wins-top-honors-at-the-bobs-online-activism-award/a-16794165 (accessed March 1, 2015).

14 Li Chengpeng, "Patriotism with Chinese characteristics," *New York Times*, May 25, 2012. Available at http://www.nytimes.com/2012/05/26/opinion/

patriotism-with-chinese-characteristics.html?pagewanted=all (accessed March 1, 2015).

15 李承鹏、刘晓新、吴策力,《中国足球内幕》, 江苏人民出版社, 2010年1月。[Li Chengpeng, Liu Xiaoxin, and Wu Celi, *China Soccer: The Inside Story* (Nanjing: Jiangsu People's Publishing Ltd., 2010).]

16 Li Chengpeng's Weibo account is available at http://www.weibo.com/lichengpeng (accessed February 27, 2014).

17 李承鹏,《全世界人民都知道》, 北京: 新星出版社, 2013年1月。[Li Chengpeng, *The Whole World Knows* (Beijing: New Star Press, 2013).]

18 David Wertime, "Did a Chinese safety official just get caught smiling at a horrific accident scene?," *Tea Leaf Nation* (website), August 27, 2012. Available at http://www.tealeafnation.com/2012/08/did-a-chinese-safety-official-just-get-caught-smiling-at-a-horrific-accident-scene/ (accessed March 1, 2015).

19 "China 'smiling official' Yang Dacai jailed for 14 years," BBC News (website), September 4, 2013. Available at http://www.bbc.co.uk/news/world-asia-china-23956170 (accessed March 1, 2015).

20 Yueran Zhang, "Tax cuts in China! But what are the consequences?," *Tea Leaf Nation* (website), August 7, 2013. Available at http://www.tealeafnation.com/2013/08/will-chinas-tax-reform-have-unintended-consequences/ (accessed March 1, 2015).

21 "Whistle-blower refuses Chongqing police request to hand over sex scandal videos," *Global Times*, January 29, 2013. Available at http://www.globaltimes.cn/content/758911.shtml (accessed March 1, 2015).

22 Andrew Jacobs, "Chinese blogger thrives as muckraker," *New York Times*, February 5, 2013. Available at http://www.nytimes.com/2013/02/06/world/asia/chinese-blogger-thrives-in-role-of-muckraker.html?_r=0 (accessed March 1, 2015).

23 Nadine DeNinno, "Lei Zhengfu: former Chinese official's sex tape leaks, journalist Zhu Ruifeng claims to have others," *International Business Times*, November 27, 2012. Available at http://www.ibtimes.com/lei-zhengfu-former-chinese-officials-sex-tape-leaks-journalist-zhu-ruifeng-claims-have-others-903156 (accessed March 1, 2015).

24 Andrew Jacobs, "Chinese blogger thrives as muckraker," *New York Times*, February 5, 2013. Available at http://www.nytimes.com/2013/02/06/world/asia/chinese-blogger-thrives-in-role-of-muckraker.html?_r=0 (accessed March 1, 2015).

25 "Whistle-blower refuses Chongqing police request to hand over sex scandal videos," *Global Times*, January 29, 2013. Available at http://www.globaltimes.cn/content/758911.shtml (accessed March 1, 2015).

26 Andrew Jacobs, "Chinese officials find misbehavior now carries cost," *New York Times*, December 25, 2012. Available at http://www.nytimes.com/2012/12/26/world/asia/corrupt-chinese-officials-draw-unusual-publicity.html?pagewanted=all (accessed March 1, 2015).

27 Chang Meng, "Whistle-blower weathers the storm," *Global Times*,

February 7, 2013. Available at http://www.globaltimes.cn/content/760706. shtml (accessed March 13, 2015).

28 "Shandong official probed after 'divorce promise' leaked online," Xinhua (news agency), November 30, 2012. Available at http://news. xinhuanet.com/english/china/2012-11/30/c_132011170.htm (accessed March 1, 2015).

29 Available at http://fenlei.baike.com/中国落马官员/ (accessed March 1, 2015).

2. Censorship Is the Mother of Subversion

1 Many people call the "Golden Shield Project" the "Great Firewall." However, others say the former appears to be geared more toward surveillance, while the latter refers mainly to censorship of content. The extent to which these terms are interchangeable, overlapping categories, or mutually exclusive is a subject of debate.

2 "The great firewall: the art of concealment," *The Economist*, April 6, 2013. Available at http://www.economist.com/news/special-report/21574631-chinese-screening-online-material-abroad-becoming-ever-more-sophisticated (accessed March 1, 2015).

3 Charles Custer, "The demise of Sina Weibo: censorship or evolution?," *Forbes*, February 4, 2014. Available at http://www.forbes.com/sites/ccuster/2014/02/04/the-demise-of-sina-weibo-censorship-or-evolution/ (accessed March 1, 2015).

4 Damian Grammaticas, "Woman jailed over Twitter post," BBC News (website), November 18, 2010. Available at http://www.bbc.co.uk/news/world-asia-pacific-11784603 (accessed March 1, 2015).

5 Perry Link, "China: the anaconda in the chandelier," *New York Review of Books*, April 11, 2002. Available at http://www.nybooks.com/articles/archives/2002/apr/11/china-the-anaconda-in-the-chandelier/ (accessed March 1, 2015).

6 Gary King, Jennifer Pan, and Margaret Roberts, "Reverse engineering Chinese censorship through randomized experimentation and participant observation," *Science* cccxlv/6199 (2014), pp. 1–10. Available at http://gking.harvard.edu/files/gking/files/experiment_0.pdf (accessed March 1, 2015).

7 "Internet information service management rules (opinion-seeking version of revision draft)," *China Copyright and Media* (blog), June 7, 2012. Available at http://chinacopyrightandmedia.wordpress.com/2012/06/07/explanation-concerning-the-internet-information-service-management-rules-opinion-seeking-version-of-revision-draft/ (accessed March 1, 2015). 白净，"从《互联网信息服务管理办法（修订草案）》看中国互联网管制趋势"，《香港电台传媒透视》，2013年8月12日。[Bai Jing, "See China's internet management strengthening trend from 'internet information services management methods (revised version),'" Radio Television Hong

Kong: Media Digest (website), August 12, 2013.] Available at http://rthk.hk/mediadigest/20130812_76_123013.html (accessed March 1, 2015).

8 "National People's Congress Standing Committee decision concerning strengthening network information protection," *China Copyright and Media* (blog), December 28, 2012. Available at http://chinacopyrightandmedia.wordpress.com/2012/12/28/national-peoples-congress-standing-committee-decision-concerning-strengthening-network-information-protection/ (accessed March 1, 2015).

9 "Thou shalt not kill: turning off the entire internet is a nuclear option best not exercised," *The Economist*, April 6, 2013. Available at http://www.economist.com/news/special-report/21574633-turning-entire-internet-nuclear-option-best-not-exercised-thou-shalt-not-kill (accessed March 1, 2015).

10 Jason Ng, "Weibo keyword un-blocking is not a victory against censorship," *Tea Leaf Nation* (website), June 21, 2013. Available at http://www.tealeafnation.com/2013/06/its-confirmed-weibo-censors-are-treating-non-chinese-users-differently/ (accessed March 1, 2015).

11 Tania Branigan, "China blocks Twitter, Flickr and Hotmail ahead of Tiananmen anniversary," *Guardian*, June 2, 2009. Available at http://www.theguardian.com/technology/2009/jun/02/twitter-china (accessed March 1, 2015).

12 Joshua Lipes, Xin Yu and Ping Chen, "Microblogging services halted," Radio Free Asia (website), March 2, 2010. Available at http://www.rfa.org/english/news/china/microblogging-03022010172017.html (accessed March 1, 2015).

13 Gady Epstein, "Sina Weibo," *Forbes*, March 3, 2011. Available at http://www.forbes.com/global/2011/0314/features-charles-chao-twitter-fanfou-china-sina-weibo.html (accessed March 1, 2015).

14 "Sina Weibo user number soars," SINA English (website), March 3, 2011. Available at http://english.sina.com/technology/p/2011/0302/362446.html (accessed March 1, 2015).

15 "SINA reports second quarter 2011 financial results," PR Newswire (website), August 17, 2011. Available at http://www.prnewswire.com/news-releases/sina-reports-second-quarter-2011-financial-results-127967183.html (accessed March 1, 2015). "32nd statistical report on internet development in China," China Internet Network Information Center (website), January 2014. Available at http://www.cnnic.net.cn/hlwfzyj/hlwxzbg/hlwtjbg/201401/P020140116395418429515.pdf (accessed March 1, 2015). Steven Millward, "Sina Weibo: we're still seeing growth, now up to 60.2 million daily active users," Tech in Asia (website), November 13, 2013. Available at http://sg.finance.yahoo.com/news/sina-weibo-still-seeing-growth-094511627.html (accessed March 1, 2015).

16 Lina Yang, "Beijing requires real names in microblog registration," Xinhua (news agency), December 16, 2011. Available at http://news.xinhuanet.com/english/china/2011-12/16/c_131310381.htm (accessed March 1, 2015).

17 David Caragliano, "Why China's real-name micro-blog rules do not work," *Tea Leaf Nation* (website), March 25, 2013. Available at http://www.tealeafnation.com/2013/03/why-chinas-real-name-micro-blog-rules-do-not-work/ (accessed March 1, 2015).

18 Liz Carter, "How China's 'reincarnation party' takes aim at online censors," *Tea Leaf Nation* (website), September 28, 2012. Available at http://www.tealeafnation.com/2012/09/how-chinas-reincarnation-party-takes-aim-at-online-censors/ (accessed March 1, 2015).

19 Ginger Huang, "A reckoning for Weibo," *World of Chinese*, March 16, 2012. Available at http://www.theworldofchinese.com/2012/03/d-day-for-real-name-registration-on-weibo-arrives/ (accessed March 1, 2015).

20 Rachel Lu, "A small victory in Chinese web's guerrilla war against army privilege," *Tea Leaf Nation* (website), April 29, 2013. Available at http://www.tealeafnation.com/2013/04/a-small-victory-in-chinese-webs-guerrilla-war-against-army-privilege/ (accessed March 1, 2015).

21 Rebecca MacKinnon, *Consent of the Networked: The Worldwide Struggle for Internet Freedom* (New York: Basic Books, 2012).

22 Gady Epstein, "A giant cage," *The Economist*, April 6, 2013. Available at http://www.economist.com/news/special-report/21574628-internet-was-expected-help-democratise-china-instead-it-has-enabled (accessed March 1, 2015).

23 Jon Sullivan, "China's Weibo: is faster different?," *New Media & Society* xvi/1 (February 2013), pp. 24–37. Available at http://nms.sagepub.com/content/16/1/24 (accessed March 1, 2015).

24 King, Pan, and Roberts, "Reverse engineering Chinese censorship."

25 Anonymous and Liz Carter, *The Grass-mud Horse Lexicon: Classic Netizen Language* (e-book), ed. Anne Henochowicz [published by the *China Digital Times*, 2013].

26 Quoted in Liz Carter, "What do you see in the Hong Kong protests?," *A Big Enough Forest* (blog), October 3, 2014. Available at http://www.abigenoughforest.net/blog/2014/10/3/what-do-you-see-in-the-hong-kong-protests.html (accessed March 1, 2015).

27 Jeffrey Wasserstrom, *China in the 21st Century: What Everyone Needs to Know* (2010; 2nd edn., New York: Oxford University Press, 2013), p. 113.

28 Quoted in Liz Carter, "In Chinese eyes, vision of 'beautiful country' gains nuance," *Tea Leaf Nation* (website), June 11, 2013. Available at http://www.tealeafnation.com/2013/06/in-chinese-eyes-vision-of-beautiful-country-gains-nuance/ (accessed March 1, 2015).

29 Robert Foyle Hunwick, "Utopia website shutdown: interview with Fan Jinggang," Danwei (website), April 14, 2012. Available at http://www.danwei.com/interview-before-a-gagging-order-fan-jinggang-of-utopia/ (accessed March 1, 2015).

30 何兵，（@1215031834），"网传新出炉的乌有之乡活埋名单,200多人。我努力不够，才排到第三级。不过比崔永元强，他才混到第五级。图片已经被成人内容过滤器过滤。" [He Bing (@1215031834), "New list from

Utopia of more than 200 people to be buried alive is circulating online. I didn't work hard enough so I was relegated to Level 3. Although I did do better than Cui Yongyuan; he only made it to Level 5."] Cached version of Weibo post via Freeweibo, October 4, 2012, 08:34. Available at https://freeweibo.com/weibo/3497325626354469 (accessed March 15, 2015).

31 "西奴标本架" ["Western slaves specimen holder"], authorship and publication date unknown. Image available at http://imgs.ntdtv.com/pic/2012/10-15/p2783051a757994328.jpg (accessed March 1, 2015).

32 Hunwick, "Utopia website shutdown: interview with Fan Jinggang."

33 Ai Weiwei, "China's paid trolls: meet the 50-cent party," *New Statesman*, October 17, 2012. Available at http://www.newstatesman.com/politics/politics/2012/10/china%E2%80%99s-paid-trolls-meet-50-cent-party (accessed March 1, 2015).

34 Ibid.

35 "Wu Yangwei," Independent Chinese PEN Center (website). Available at http://www.penchinese.org/english/116-wu-yangwei (accessed March 1, 2015).

36 Quoted in Carter, "How China's 'reincarnation party' takes aim at online censors."

37 Oiwan Lam, "China: bloggers 'forced to drink tea' with police," Global Voices (website), February 19, 2013. Available at http://advocacy.globalvoicesonline.org/2013/02/19/china-bloggers-forced-to-drink-tea-with-police/ (accessed March 1, 2015).

38 Ning Hui, "Crowdsourcing activism: China's 'food delivery party,'" *Tea Leaf Nation* (website), September 11, 2013. Available at http://www.tealeafnation.com/2013/09/crowdsourcing-activism-chinas-food-delivery-party/ (accessed March 1, 2015).

39 Ibid.

40 Xiao Guozhen, "What is a same-city dinner gathering?," China Change (website), September 22, 2013. Available at http://chinachange.org/2013/09/22/what-is-a-same-city-dinner-gathering/ (accessed March 1, 2015).

3. Tectonic Shifts: Counterculture Online

1 Chris Marquis and Zoe Yang, "Diaosi: evolution of a Chinese meme," Civil China (website), July 27, 2013. Available at http://www.civilchina.org/2013/07/diaosi-evolution-of-a-chinese-meme/ (accessed March 1, 2015).

2 "2012十大流行语公布 "屌丝" 落选", 《南方都市报》, 2012年12月31日。["Top ten popular words and phrases of 2012 announced, diaosi not selected," *Southern Metropolis Daily*, December 31, 2012.] Available at https://web.archive.org/web/20130103053607/http://epaper.oeeee.com/A/html/2012-12/31/content_1786883.htm (accessed March 1, 2015).

3 Claire Zhang and David Barreda, "Hip, young, and wired: China's 'diaosi,' in charts," *Atlantic*, June 29, 2013. Available at http://www.theatlantic.com/

china/archive/2013/06/hip-young-and-wired-chinas-diaosi-in-charts/277359/ (accessed March 1, 2015).

4   Linda Chen, "Feng Xiaogang: diaosi = pubes," Sino-US.com, February 28, 2013. Available at http://www.sino-us.com/120/Feng-Xiaogang-Diaosi-Pubes.html (accessed March 1, 2015).

5   "CNNIC 2012年中国网民社交网站应用研究报告", 《中国互联网络信息中心》, 2012年12月。["CNNIC 2012 China netizen social media site app research report," China Internet Network Information Center (website), December 2012.] Available at https://www.cnnic.net.cn/hlwfzyj/hlwxzbg/sqbg/201302/P020130219611651054576.pdf (accessed March 1, 2015).

6   Marquis and Yang, "Diaosi: evolution of a Chinese meme."

7   Koh Gui Qing and Aileen Wang, "Rising home prices send China's 'rat race' scurrying underground," Reuters (news agency), January 5, 2014. Available at http://www.reuters.com/article/2014/01/05/us-china-property-basement-idUSBREA040GD20140105 (accessed March 1, 2015).

8   Leta Hong Fincher, *Leftover Women: The Resurgence of Gender Inequality in China* (London: Zed Books, 2014).

9   Kellee S. Tsai, "Private sector development and Communist resilience in China," in Martin K. Dimitrov, ed., *Why Communism Did Not Collapse* (New York: Cambridge University Press, 2013).

10   "Wealthy politicians," *The Economist*, September 28, 2013. Available at http://www.economist.com/news/china/21586883-wealthy-politicians (accessed March 1, 2015).

11   Rachel Lu, "Meet China's Beverly Hillbillies," *Foreign Policy*, October 15, 2013. Available at http://www.foreignpolicy.com/articles/2013/10/15/meet_chinas_beverly_hillbillies (accessed March 1, 2015).

12   Teng He, "'Feudal' China makes a comeback, through slang," *Tea Leaf Nation* (website), August 21, 2013. Available at http://www.tealeafnation.com/2013/08/chinese-slang/ (accessed March 1, 2015).

13   Rachel Lu, "Lifestyles of the rich and shameless – meet China's 'tuhao,'" *Tea Leaf Nation* (website), October 15, 2013. Available at http://www.tealeafnation.com/2013/10/lifestyles-of-the-rich-and-shameless-meet-chinas-tuhao/ (accessed March 1, 2015).

14   Ning Hui, "Born rich in China: explaining the disdain for 'fu'erdai,'" *Tea Leaf Nation* (website), March 9, 2013. Available at http://www.tealeafnation.com/2013/03/born-rich-in-china-explaining-the-disdain-for-fuerdai/ (accessed March 1, 2015).

15   Li Jing, "Hainan school principal, official reportedly to be charged with rapes of schoolgirls," *South China Morning Post*, May 26, 2013. Available at http://www.scmp.com/news/china/article/1246062/hainan-school-principal-official-reportedly-be-charged-rapes-schoolgirls (accessed March 1, 2015).

16   "12338", 《百度百科》。["12338," *Baidu Baike*.] Available at http://www.baike.com/wiki/12338 (accessed March 1, 2015).

17   Lotus Ruan, "Chinese hold online protest against child predators, say #GetARoomWithMeInstead," *Tea Leaf Nation* (website), May 29, 2013.

Available at http://www.tealeafnation.com/2013/05/chinese-hold-online-protest-against-child-predators-say-getaroomwithme-instead/ (accessed March 1, 2015).

18 Liu Sheng, "Hainan principal, official jailed for raping six elementary students," *Global Times*, June 21, 2013. Available at http://www.globaltimes.cn/content/790544.shtml#.UuL12Pso5pQ (accessed March 1, 2015).

19 Weibo account: Ye Haiyan (@yehaiyan1975). Available at http://weibo.com/yehaiyan1975 (accessed February 27, 2014). Tencent Weibo account: Ye Haiyan (@hooliganyan). Available at http://t.qq.com/hooliganyan (accessed February 27, 2014).

20 Twitter account: Ye Haiyan (@liumangyan). Available at https://twitter.com/liumangyan (accessed February 27, 2014).

21 Paul Mooney, "China's sex-worker warrior Ye Haiyan fights for prostitutes' rights," *Daily Beast* (website), July 31, 2012. Available at http://www.thedailybeast.com/articles/2012/07/31/china-s-sex-worker-warrior-ye-haiyan-fights-for-prostitutes-rights.html (accessed March 1, 2015).

22 Ibid.

23 Tang Yue, "Speaking up for those who inhabit a world of shadows," *China Daily*, June 5, 2012. Available at http://europe.chinadaily.com.cn/china/2012-06/05/content_15473407.htm (accessed March 1, 2015).

24 周华蕾，"'流氓燕'：性工作者站出来"，《南方周末》，2012年4月27日。[Zhou Hualei, "'Hooligan Yan': sex workers rise up," *Southern Weekly*, April 27, 2012.] Available at http://www.infzm.com/content/74630 (accessed March 1, 2015).

25 "专访艾晓明：裸露就是反抗"，《网易女人》，2013年6月25日。["Exclusive interview with Ai Xiaoming: nakedness is resistance," NetEase Lady (website), June 25, 2013.] Available at http://lady.163.com/13/0625/17/927TUDR7002626I3_all.html#p1 (accessed March 1, 2015).

26 "Ai Xiaoming speaks up for woman behind child abuse campaign," *Want China Times* (website), June 1, 2013. Available at http://www.wantchinatimes.com/news-subclass-cnt.aspx?id=20130601000096&cid=1103 (accessed March 1, 2015).

27 "专访艾晓明：裸露就是反抗"。["Exclusive interview with Ai Xiaoming: nakedness is resistance."]

28 Yaxue Cao, "Help Ye Haiyan!," China Change (website), July 6, 2013. Available at http://chinachange.org/2013/07/06/help-ye-haiyan/ (accessed March 1, 2015).

29 Yinan Zhao, "Renowned teacher admits abusing his wife," *China Daily*, September 13, 2013. Available at http://www.chinadaily.com.cn/cndy/2011-09/13/content_13670686.htm (accessed March 1, 2015).

30 Didi Kirsten Tatlow, "In China's most-watched divorce case, 3 victories, 1 defeat," *New York Times: IHT Rendezvous* (blog), February 4, 2013. Available at http://rendezvous.blogs.nytimes.com/2013/02/04/in-chinas-most-watched-divorce-case-3-victories-1-defeat/ (accessed March 1, 2015).

31 These comments were posted on the following Weibo post: Kim Lee

(@2254494161), "My back is weak after having kids. You weigh much more than me. Lydia screamed and scratched your arm to get you to stop. When you did, I got up, grabbed our passports, grabbed her, and ran to the police station." Weibo, September 5, 2011, 20:44. Available at http://www.weibo.com/2254494161/xmOjoceIq#_rnd1393359994160 (accessed March 1, 2015).

32 Kenneth Tan, "Li Yang of Crazy English to get dumped by wife?," *Shanghaiist* (blog), September 6, 2011. Available at http://shanghaiist.com/2011/09/06/li_yang_of_crazy_english_to_get_dum.php (accessed March 1, 2015).

33 "中国超两成女性遭遇家暴 反家庭暴力法刻不容缓"，《中国新闻网》，2012年3月26日。["More than 20 percent of Chinese women have encountered domestic violence, anti-domestic violence law is urgently needed," *China News Online* (website), March 26, 2012.] Available at http://gongyi.163.com/12/0326/10/7TH0I37L00933KC8.html (accessed March 1, 2015).

34 林靖，"5起诉讼 只有一起能认'家暴'"，《北京晚报》，2013年09月30日。[Lin Jing, "Of five suits only one can be considered 'domestic violence,'" *Beijing Evening News*, September 30, 2013.] Available at http://bjwb.bjd.com.cn/html/2013-09/30/content_113423.htm (accessed March 1, 2015).

35 "中国超两成女性遭遇家暴 反家庭暴力法刻不容缓"，《人民日报海外版》，2012年03月24日。["Over 20 percent of women in China experience domestic violence, anti-domestic violence law urgently needed," *People's Daily Overseas Edition*, March 24, 2012.] Available at http://news.xinhuanet.com/society/2012-03/24/c_111697108.htm (accessed March 1, 2015).

36 "苍井空、凤姐 传遭大陆封杀禁上电视"，《TVBS》，2012年4月17日。["Rumors circulate that Sola Aoi and Feng Jie banned from television in mainland China," TVBS (website), April 17, 2012.] Available at http://news.tvbs.com.tw/entry/15030 (accessed March 1, 2015). Weibo account: Sola Aoi (@1739928273). Available at http://weibo.com/u/1739928273 (accessed February 28, 2014).

37 Liz Carter, "China's animated sex ed videos just went viral, and for a good reason," *Foreign Policy*, November 5, 2013. Available at http://blog.foreignpolicy.com/posts/2013/11/05/china_s_viral_minute_long_sex_ed_videos (accessed March 1, 2015).

38 易小荷，"苍井空：无危险的反抗"《南都周刊》，2013年10月15日。[Yi Xiaohe, "Sola Aoi: Resistance without danger," *Southern Metropolis Weekly*, October 15, 2013.] Available at http://www.nbweekly.com/news/special/201310/34631.aspx (Accessed April 1, 2015).

39 "Online survey report on the work environment for China's LGBT community" (May 2013). Available at http://www.aibai.com/ebook/library/ebook_aibai/download/2013/8/16/online_survey_report_on_the_work_environment_for_chinas_lgbt_community_en.pdf (accessed March 1, 2015). Tabitha Spellman, "Where humiliation is normal—being LGBT in the Chinese workplace," *Tea Leaf Nation* (website), September 9, 2013. Available at http://www.tealeafnation.com/2013/09/where-humiliation-is-normal-being-lgbt-in-the-chinese-workplace/ (accessed March 1, 2015).

40 Liu Yunyun, "Quiet pink revolution in dark before dawn?," *Beijing Review*, December 26, 2005. Available at http://www.bjreview.cn/EN/En-2005/05-51-e/china-1.htm (accessed March 1, 2015).

41 David Wertime, "A case study of Chinese netizen attitude towards homosexuality," *Tea Leaf Nation* (website), April 26, 2012. Available at http://www.tealeafnation.com/2012/04/a-case-study-of-chinese-netizen-attitude-towards-homosexuality/ (accessed March 1, 2015). "你对黄耀明承认自己是同性恋怎么看？"《新浪调查》，2012年4月24日。["What do you think about Anthony Wang admitting that he is homosexual?," Sina Surveys (website), April 24, 2012.] Available at http://survey.ent.sina.com.cn/result/68462.html (accessed March 1, 2015).

42 David Wertime, "Online, being gay in China gets much 'respect,' but less 'acceptance,'" *Tea Leaf Nation* (website), May 19, 2013. Available at http://www.tealeafnation.com/2012/05/online-being-gay-in-china-gets-much-respect-but-less-acceptance/ (accessed March 1, 2015).

43 Liz Carter, "On Chinese Valentine's Day, two men get engaged while netizens cheer," *Tea Leaf Nation* (website), August 24, 2012. Available at http://www.tealeafnation.com/2012/08/on-chinese-valentines-day-two-men-get-engaged-while-netizens-cheer/ (accessed March 1, 2015).

44 "见证'两个老头的爱情'老年男同性恋者甜蜜'完婚'[组图]"，《中国新闻网》，2013年1月31日。["Standing witness to the sweet 'wedding' of the two elderly gay men of 'two old guys in love' (slideshow)," *China News Online* (website), January 31, 2013.] Available at http://www.china.com.cn/photochina/2013-01/31/content_27846948.htm (accessed March 1, 2015).

45 A cached version of Mr. Yang and Mr. He's Weibo post is available at https://freeweibo.com/weibo/3540629034221659 (accessed March 1, 2015).

46 "北京'两个老头'举办同性婚礼 遭儿子闹场(组图)"《淡蓝网》，2013年1月31日。["Beijing 'two old guys in love' hold gay wedding, son disrupts ceremony (slideshow)," Danlan Online, January 31, 2013.] Available at http://www.danlan.org/disparticle_42702_2_1.htm (accessed March 1, 2015).

47 Steve Millward, "Born this way: China gets its first gay flirting app, Blued," Tech in Asia (website), August 23, 2012. Available at http://www.techinasia.com/blued-gay-chinese-flirting-app/#fn:1 (accessed March 1, 2015).

48 Steve Millward, "Blued, a gay dude flirting app from China, picks up 2 million users and plans lesbian app next," Tech in Asia (website), December 2, 2013. Available at http://www.techinasia.com/blued-gay-flirting-app-from-china-hits-2-million-users/ (accessed March 1, 2015). Jordan Crook, "Grindr's Joel Simkhai announces 4M users, 1M daily uniques, and weighs in on the Skout disaster," TechCrunch (website), June 17, 2012. Available at http://techcrunch.com/2012/06/17/grindrs-joel-simkhai-announces-4m-users-1m-daily-uniques-and-weighs-in-on-the-skout-disaster/ (accessed March 1, 2015).

Sonja Cheung, "'Dream come true' Chinese gay dating app Blued raises $30 million," *Wall Street Journal: Venture Capital Dispatch* (blog), November 5, 2014. Available at http://blogs.wsj.com/venturecapital/2014/11/05/dream-come-true-chinese-gay-dating-app-blued-raises-30-million/ (accessed March 1, 2015).

49 David Wertime, "In online poll, a majority support gay marriage in China," *Tea Leaf Nation* (website), February 28, 2013. Available at http://www.tealeafnation.com/2013/02/in-online-poll-a-majority-support-gay-marriage-in-china/ (accessed March 1, 2015). "你怎么看百余同性恋父母呼吁修改婚姻法？"，《新浪调查》，2013年2月27日。["How do you feel about PFLAG China's call to change the marriage law?," Sina Surveys (website), February 27, 2013.] Available at http://survey.news.sina.com.cn/result/76781.html (accessed March 1, 2015).

50 "Chinese Valentine's Day, our gay day!," Xinhua (news agency), August 13, 2013. Available at http://news.xinhuanet.com/english/china/2013-08/13/c_132627803.htm (accessed March 1, 2015).

51 Rachel Lu, "Joke about gay romance on Chinese New Year gala lights up blogosphere," *Tea Leaf Nation* (website), February 10, 2013. Available at http://www.tealeafnation.com/2013/02/joke-about-gay-romance-on-chinas-new-year-gala-lights-up-blogosphere/ (accessed March 1, 2015).

52 Wang's post is available at http://weibo.com/1793285524/AkBclD5XL (accessed March 1, 2015). Li's post is available at http://weibo.com/2103206685/AkIXGj7yg (accessed March 1, 2015).

53 微博搜索："耽美"。[Weibo search: "Danmei."] Available at http://s.weibo.com/user/%25E8%2580%25BD%25E7%25BE%25E8&Refer=weibo_user (searched February 28, 2015).

54 Weibo account: DanmeiFanficResources (@2477002587). Available at http://weibo.com/u/2477002587 (accessed February 28, 2014).

55 Yang Jingjie, "SARFT tightens online video rules content," *Global Times*, July 11, 2012. Available at http://www.globaltimes.cn/content/720327.shtml (accessed March 1, 2015).

56 "广电总局将加强电视上星综合频道节目管理"，《宣传司》，2011年10月25日。["State administration of press, publication, radio, and television to strengthen television overall channel program management," Publicity Department (website), October 25, 2011.] Available at http://www.sarft.gov.cn/articles/2011/10/25/20111025170755801010.html (accessed March 1, 2015).

57 Pete Sweeney, "China to restrict satellite TV stations to one foreign program," Reuters (news agency), October 20, 2013. Available at http://www.reuters.com/article/2013/10/21/us-china-tv-idUSBRE99K01I20131021 (accessed March 1, 2015).

58 "对歌唱类选拔节目实行调控　为观众提供丰富多彩电视节目"，《宣传管理司》，2013年7月24日。["Adjustments to singing competition programs to provide audiences with more abundant and excellent television programs," Publicity Management Department (website), July 24, 2013.] Available at http://www.sarft.gov.cn/articles/2013/07/24/20130724184549270586.html (accessed March 1, 2015).

59 Rachel Lu, "Director reveals mystery of China's film censorship system on Weibo," *Tea Leaf Nation* (website), September 27, 2012. Available at http://www.tealeafnation.com/2012/09/director-reveals-mystery-of-chinas-film-censorship-system-on-weibo/ (accessed March 1, 2015).

60 Lilian Lin, "China cracks down on televised singing competitions," *Wall Street Journal: China Real Time* (blog), July 30, 2013. Available at http://blogs.wsj.com/chinarealtime/2013/07/30/china-cracks-down-on-televised-singing-competitions/ (accessed March 1, 2015).

61 王地、康锦、张晓军，"妙龄少女热衷创作'耽美'小说'软色情'危害大"，《检察日报》，2011年11月28日。[Wang Di, Kang Jin, and Zhang Xiaojin, "Girls in prime of youth obsessed with creating 'danmei' novels, 'softcore pornography' very harmful," *Justice Online*, November 28, 2011.] Available at http://npc.people.com.cn/GB/16406788.html (accessed March 1, 2015).

62 "视频：天天故事会：神秘写手落网记[超级新闻场]"，《优酷》，2014年4月3日。["Video: daily stories: how the mysterious writers were caught (super news spot)]," Youku, April 3, 2014.] Available at http://v.youku.com/v_show/id_XNjkzNzgxMDA4.html?qq-pf-to=pcqq.c2c (accessed March 1, 2015).

63 "《神探夏洛克》回归 揭秘BBC全球特供的中国嫁妆"，《南方都市报》，2014年01月03日。["*Sherlock* returns, reveals BBC's gift to China of global offering," *Southern Metropolis Daily*, January 3, 2014.] Available at http://news.xinhuanet.com/ent/2014-01/03/c_125952474.htm (accessed March 1, 2015).

64 Xiaoqing Cheng, *Sherlock in Shanghai: Stories of Crime and Detection* (Honolulu: University of Hawaii Press, 2007). "New 'Sherlock Holmes' translation gets a classical Chinese twist," *Global Times*, November 12, 2012. Available at http://www.globaltimes.cn/content/743851.shtml (accessed March 1, 2015).

65 张媛，"夏洛克效应：英剧在中国刮起收视旋风"，《前瞻网》，2013年10月23日。[Zhang Yuan, "The Sherlock effect: viewership of British shows increasing dramatically in China," Qianzhan.com, October 23, 2013.] Available at http://www.qianzhan.com/analyst/detail/220/131023-d2a379b8.html (accessed March 1, 2015).

66 微博搜索："卷福"。[Weibo search: "Curly Fu."] Available at http://s.weibo.com/user/%25E5%258D%25B7%25E7%25A6%258F&Refer=weibo_user (searched February 28, 2015).

67 Weibo account: IanTees_CurlyFuHiddleston (@2610642413). Available at http://www.weibo.com/u/2610642413 (accessed February 28, 2014).

68 Weibo account: MTSlash (@mtslash). Available at http://www.weibo.com/mtslash (accessed February 28, 2014). Website: MTSlash. Available at http://www.mtslash.com/forum.php (accessed February 28, 2014).

4. Not in My Backyard: From Screens to Streets

1 Guobin Yang, *The Power of the Internet in China* (New York: Columbia University Press, 2011), p. 240.

2 "杭州一幼儿园运动会现'保卫钓鱼岛'比赛(组图)", 《凤凰网》, 2012年11月15日。["Hangzhou kindergarten field day includes 'protect the Diaoyu Islands' competition (slideshow)," Ifeng.com, November 15, 2012.] Available at http://news.ifeng.com/mainland/special/diaoyudaozhengduan/content-3/detail_2012_11/15/19193867_0.shtml (accessed March 1, 2015).

3 Liz Carter, "Chinese literature textbooks modified to curb 'deep thinking,'" *Tea Leaf Nation* (website), September 4, 2013. Available at http://www.tealeafnation.com/2013/09/goodbye-lu-xun-official-textbooks-remove-father-of-chinese-literature-to-prevent-deep-thinking/ (accessed March 1, 2015).

4 "人教版语文教材删鲁迅文章专家称过于深刻", 《河南商报》, 2013年09月04日。["People's Education Press language and literature teaching materials delete Lu Xun article, expert says too deep," *Henan Business Daily*, September 4, 2013.] Available at http://news.xinhuanet.com/overseas/2013-09/04/c_125319817.htm (accessed March 1, 2015).

5 Liz Carter, "China's propaganda department rolls out recommended reading list, parents reject 'brainwashing' books," *Tea Leaf Nation* (website), July 16, 2013. Available at http://www.tealeafnation.com/2013/07/china-rolls-out-recommended-reading-list-parents-reject-brainwashing-books/ (accessed March 1, 2015).

6 Wen Ya, "Teacher challenges textbook errors," *Global Times*, December 4, 2013. Available at http://www.globaltimes.cn/content/829930.shtml#.UtH9TfRDvXY (accessed March 1, 2015).

7 杜羽, "语文教材出错了？", 《光明日报》, 2013年11月25日。[Du Yu, "Were there mistakes in the language and literature teaching materials?," *Guangming Daily*, November 25, 2013.] Available at http://epaper.gmw.cn/gmrb/html/2013-11/25/nw.D110000gmrb_20131125_3-06.htm (accessed March 1, 2015). "人教社为语文教材出错致歉 相关教材不会召回", 《南方周末》, 2013年12月4日。["People's Education Press apologizes for mistakes in language and literature teaching materials, relevant teaching materials will not be recalled," *Southern Weekly*, December 4, 2014.] Available at http://www.infzm.com/content/96423 (accessed March 1, 2015).

8 "国民教育中心反击洗脑指摘", 《昔日东方》, 2012年7月13日。["National education center strikes back against brainwashing accusation," *Oriental Daily*, July 13, 2012.] Available at http://orientaldaily.on.cc/cnt/news/20120713/00176_046.html (accessed March 1, 2015).

9 @Hexiefarm, "可爱的香港小朋友 #七一草泥马节 #hk71"。[@Hexiefarm, "Cute Hong Kong Kids #71GrassMudHorseDay #hk71".] Twitter, July 1, 2012, 10:28. Available at https://twitter.com/hexiefarm/status/219452337339633664/photo/1/large (accessed March 1, 2015).

10 Alexis Lai, "'National education' raises furor in Hong Kong," CNN, July 30, 2012. Available at http://www.cnn.com/2012/07/30/world/asia/hong-kong-national-education-controversy/ (accessed March 1, 2015).

11 Quoted in Liz Carter, "What do you see in the Hong Kong protests?," *A Big Enough Forest* (blog), October 3, 2014. Available at http://www.abigenoughforest.net/blog/2014/10/3/what-do-you-see-in-the-hong-kong-protests.html (accessed March 1, 2015).

12 "Chinese anger over pollution becomes main cause of social unrest," Bloomberg (news agency), March 6, 2013. Available at http://www.bloomberg.com/news/2013-03-06/pollution-passes-land-grievances-as-main-spark-of-china-protests.html (accessed March 1, 2015).

13 Shan Juan and An Baijie, "Study reaffirms 'cancer villages,'" *China Daily*, August 8, 2013. Available at http://usa.chinadaily.com.cn/china/2013-08/08/content_16878735.htm (accessed March 1, 2015).

14 Josh Chin and Brian Spegele, "China's bad earth," *Wall Street Journal*, July 27, 2013. Available at http://www.wsj.com/articles/SB10001424127887323829104578624010648228142 (accessed March 1, 2015).

15 John Kaiman, "Inside China's 'cancer villages,'" *Guardian*, June 4, 2013. Available at http://www.theguardian.com/world/2013/jun/04/china-villages-cancer-deaths (accessed March 1, 2015).

16 David Wertime, "China's state-run media shares powerful map of 'cancer villages' creeping inland," China File (website), February 22, 2014. Available at http://www.chinafile.com/chinas-state-run-media-shares-powerful-map-cancer-villages-creeping-inland (accessed March 1, 2015).

17 张向永，"1条洪河流出8个癌症高发村 灾难来自何方？———来自河南省吕店乡的污染调查"，《人民网》，2004年12月7日。[Zhang Xiangyong, "Eight villages with high rates of cancer along one big river, what is the source of this disaster? An investigation into the pollution in Lvdianxiang, Henan province," *People's Daily Online*, December 7, 2004.] Available at http://webcache.googleusercontent.com/search?q=cache:q8PF6kEnHTgJ:www.people.com.cn/GB/huanbao/35525/3037798.html+&cd=1&hl=en&ct=clnk&gl=us (accessed March 1, 2015).

18 Brian Spegele, "Sichuan protest turns violent," *Wall Street Journal: China Real Time* (blog), July 2, 2012. Available at http://blogs.wsj.com/chinarealtime/2012/07/02/sichuan-protest-turns-violent/ (accessed March 1, 2015).

19 Quoted in Anne Henochowicz, "Shifang: a study in contrasts," *China Digital Times*, July 6, 2012. Available at http://chinadigitaltimes.net/2012/07/shifang-a-study-contrasts/ (accessed March 1, 2015).

20 Rachel Lu, "Dramatic photos – NIMBY protest turns bloody in western China," *Tea Leaf Nation* (website), July 3, 2012. Available at http://www.tealeafnation.com/2012/07/dramatic-photos-nimby-protest-turns-bloody-in-western-china/ (accessed March 1, 2015).

21 Qian Gang, "China's malformed media sphere," China Media Project (website), July 11, 2012. Available at http://cmp.hku.hk/2012/07/11/25293/ (accessed March 1, 2015).

22 See Mark McDonald, "Taking it to the street in China," *New York Times: IHT Rendezvous* (blog), July 29, 2012. Available at http://rendezvous.blogs. nytimes.com/2012/07/29/taking-it-to-the-street-in-china/ (accessed March 1, 2015).

23 Jane Perlez, "Waste project is abandoned following protests in China," *New York Times*, July 28, 2012. Available at http://www.nytimes. com/2012/07/29/world/asia/after-protests-in-qidong-china-plans-for-water-discharge-plant-are-abandoned.html (accessed March 1, 2015).

24 John Ruwitch, "China cancels waste project after protests turn violent," Reuters (news agency), July 28, 2012. Available at http://www.reuters.com/ article/2012/07/28/us-china-environment-protest-idUSBRE86R02Y20120728 (accessed March 1, 2015).

25 "US embassy Beijing air quality monitor," Embassy of the United States: Beijing, China (website). Available at http://beijing.usembassy-china.org. cn/aqirecent3.html (accessed March 1, 2015).

26 Austin Ramzy, "Conflict in the air: US vows to keep reporting on pollution in China," *Time*, June 6, 2012. Available at http://world.time. com/2012/06/06/conflict-in-the-air-u-s-will-keep-reporting-on-pollution-in-china/ (accessed March 1, 2015).

27 "Guo Feixiong and Sun Desheng indictment," China Change (website), July 7, 2014. Available at http://chinachange.org/2014/07/07/guo-feixiong-and-sun-desheng-indictment/ (accessed March 1, 2015).

28 David Bandurski, "A New Year's greeting gets the axe in China," China Media Project (website), January 3, 2013. Available at http://cmp.hku. hk/2013/01/03/30247/ (accessed March 1, 2015).

29 戴志勇，"中国梦、宪政梦"，《香港文汇报》，2013年1月03日。 [Dai Zhiyong, "The Chinese dream, the dream of constitutionalism," *Wenweipo*, January 3, 2013.] Available at http://info.wenweipo.com/index. php?action-viewnews-itemid-59878 (accessed March 1, 2015).

30 "Charter 08," Human Rights in China (website), December 9, 2008. Available at http://www.hrichina.org/en/content/3203 (accessed March 1, 2015).

31 "'Struggling' against constitutionalism," China Media Project (website), September 25, 2013. Available at http://cmp.hku.hk/2013/09/25/34196/ (accessed March 1, 2015).

32 凯文，"《南方周末》新年献词遭广东省委宣传部长越权篡改"，《rfi 华语》，2013年1月3日。[Kai Wen, "*Southern Weekly* New Year's greeting changed by Guangdong provincial Party committee publicity department chief in violation of rules," Radio France Internationale, Chinese Edition (website), January 3, 2013.] Available at http://cn.rfi.fr/中国/20130103-《南方周末》新年献词遭广东省委宣传部长越权篡改/ (accessed March 1, 2015).

33 Rachel Lu, "Online and off, social media users go to war for freedom of press in China," *Tea Leaf Nation* (website), January 7, 2013. Available at http://www.tealeafnation.com/2013/01/online-and-off-social-media-users-go-to-war-for-freedom-of-press-in-china/ (accessed March 1, 2015).

34 Yao's post is available at http://weibo.com/1266321801/zdl7c3yVs (accessed March 1, 2015).

35 Quoted in David Bandurski, "Inside the *Southern Weekly* incident," China Media Project (website), January 7, 2013. Available at http://cmp.hku.hk/2013/01/07/30402/ (accessed March 1, 2015).

36 曹国星，"《南方周末》重压下分裂：高层妥协 采编酝酿罢工"，《rfi 华语》，2013年1月7日。[Cao Guoxing, "*Southern Weekly* fractures under heavy pressure: higher-level workers seek compromise, editorial and sourcing staff strike," Radio France Internationale, Chinese Edition (website), January 7, 2013.] Available at http://cn.rfi.fr/中国/20130106-《南方周末》重压下分裂：高层妥协-采编酝酿罢工/ (accessed March 1, 2015).

37 westmoon (@westmoon), "南方周末经济部11人采编人员罢工声明"。[westmoon (@westmoon), "*Southern Weekly* economics department 11 editors statement on strike."] Twitter, January 6, 2013, 08:33. Available at https://twitter.com/westmoon/status/287929829762928640/photo/1 (accessed March 1, 2015).

38 Tom Bannister, "Photos: protestors in Guangzhou come out in support of *Southern Weekly* and press freedom," *Shanghaiist* (blog), January 7, 2013. Available at http://shanghaiist.com/2013/01/07/guangzhou-southern-weekend-protest.php#photo-1 (accessed March 1, 2015).

39 "南方周末'致读者'实在令人深思"，《环球时报》，2013年1月7日。["*Southern Weekly*'s 'To readers' truly makes people consider," *Global Times*, January 7, 2013.] Available at http://news.xinhuanet.com/politics/2013-01/07/c_114280461.htm (accessed March 1, 2015).

40 Amy Li and Liu Yi, "China censorship storm spreads, Beijing paper publisher resigns in protest," *South China Morning Post*, January 9, 2013. Available at http://www.scmp.com/news/china/article/1123824/china-censorship-storm-spreads-beijing-paper-publisher-resigns-protest (accessed March 1, 2015). "《南方周末》新年致辞事件时间轴"，《深度故事》，2013 年 1 月 23 日。["*Southern Weekly* New Year's greeting incident timeline," China Current (website), January 23, 2013.] Available at http://www.cncurrent.com/?p=704 (accessed March 1, 2015).

41 "China censor row paper *Southern Weekly* back on stands," BBC News (website), January 10, 2013. Available at http://www.bbc.co.uk/news/world-asia-china-20968170 (accessed March 1, 2015).

5. I Fought the Law

1 Emily Parker, *Now I Know Who My Comrades Are: Voices from the Internet Underground* (New York: Farrar, Straus & Giroux, 2014), p. 68.

2 谢铭，"唐慧 被劳教的上访妈妈"，《南方周末》，2012年8月23日 [Xie Ming, "Tang Hui: the Petitioning Mother Sent to Re-education Through

Labor Camp," *Southern Weekly*, August 23, 2012.] Available at http://www. infzm.com/content/79993 (accessed March 25, 2015).

3   Xi Chen, *Social Protest and Contentious Authoritarianism in China* (Cambridge: Cambridge University Press, 2014), p. 46.

4   Quoted in Yueran Zhang, "Can one woman's case change a 70-year-old system of injustice?," *Tea Leaf Nation* (website), August 21, 2012. Available at http://www.tealeafnation.com/2012/08/can-one-womans-case-change-a-70-year-old-system-of-injustice/ (accessed March 1, 2015).

5   Quoted in Lotus Ruan, "China's 'petitioning mother' wins appeal: netizens ask, 'Is this victory?'," *Tea Leaf Nation* (website), July 17, 2013. Available at http://www.tealeafnation.com/2013/07/chinas-petitioning-mother-wins-appeal-netizens-ask-is-this-victory/ (accessed March 1, 2015).

6   Quoted in " '上访妈妈' 发声明: 我不满意", 《中国网事综合》, 2014年9月5日。["'Petitioning mother' makes statement: I am not satisfied," China Internet Affairs Comprehensive, September 5, 2014.] Available at http:// www.zhongguowangshi.com/info.aspx?id=65267 (accessed March 17, 2015).

7   Quoted ibid.

8   Yueran Zhang, "China's 'urban enforcers' caught in a vicious cycle," *Tea Leaf Nation* (website), June 24, 2013. Available at http://www.tealeafnation. com/2013/06/chinas-urban-enforcers-caught-in-a-vicious-cycle/ (accessed March 17, 2015).

9   Teng Biao, "Teng Biao: defense in the second trial of Xia Junfeng case," trans. Yaxue Cao (and others), *Seeing Red in China* (blog), February 18, 2013. Available at http://chinachange.org/2013/02/18/teng-biao-defense-in-the-second-trial-of-xia-junfeng-case/ (accessed March 17, 2015).

10   潘珊菊, "湖南临武县城管被曝打死瓜农", 《京华时报》, 2013年 07月18日。[Pan Shanju, "Hunan Linwu county chengguan revealed to have beaten melon vendor to death," *Beijing Times*, July 18, 2013.] Available at http://epaper.jinghua.cn/html/2013-07/18/content_10433.htm (accessed March 17, 2015).

11   "云南警方通报躲猫猫事件 称李玩游戏发生意外", 《新浪新闻》, 2009年02月21日。["Yunnan police report hide-and-seek incident, say Li had accident while playing game," *Sina News*, February 21, 2009.] Available at http://news.sina.com.cn/c/2009-02-21/032717258307.shtml (accessed March 17, 2015).

12   Quoted in Jiabao Du, "Watermelon vendor's death triggers backlash against China's urban management officers," *Tea Leaf Nation* (website), July 22, 2013. Available at http://www.tealeafnation.com/2013/07/watermelon-vendors-death-triggers-anger-against-chinas-urban-management-officers/ (accessed March 1, 2015).

13   Quoted ibid.

14   Quoted ibid.

15   Quoted ibid.

16   Li Chengpeng, "Li Chengpeng's essay translated: watermelon vendor died pursuing the Chinese dream," *Telegraph*, July 19, 2013. Available at http://www.telegraph.co.uk/news/worldnews/asia/china/10190914/ Li-Chengpengs-essay-translated-watermelon-vendor-died-pursuing-the-Chinese-dream.html (accessed March 1, 2015).

17 Quoted in Jiabao Du, "Watermelon vendor's death triggers backlash against China's urban management officers," *Tea Leaf Nation* (website), July 22, 2013. Available at http://www.tealeafnation.com/2013/07/watermelon-vendors-death-triggers-anger-against-chinas-urban-management-officers/ (accessed March 1, 2015).

18 Xu Zhiyong, "China needs a new citizens' movement," Human Rights in China (website), July 23, 2012. Available at http://www.hrichina.org/en/crf/article/6205 (accessed March 1, 2015).

19 Teng Biao, "A Hole to Bury You," *Wall Street Journal*, December 28, 2010. Available at http://online.wsj.com/news/articles/SB10001424052970203731 004576045152244293970 (accessed March 25, 2015).

20 "Liu Ping's final statement at trial," Human Rights in China (website), December 5, 2013. Available at http://www.hrichina.org/en/press-work/hric-bulletin/liu-pings-final-statement-trial (accessed March 1, 2015).

21 Ding Jiaxi, "To be a citizen who speaks up and has an attitude: lawyer Ding Jiaxi speaks from prison," China Change (website), April 6, 2014. Available at http://chinachange.org/2014/04/06/to-be-a-citizen-who-speaks-up-and-has-an-attitude-lawyer-ding-jiaxi-speaks-from-prison/ (accessed March 1, 2015).

22 Xu Zhiyong, "For freedom, justice and love – my closing statement to the court," China Change (website), January 22, 2014. Available at http://chinachange.org/2014/01/23/for-freedom-justice-and-love-my-closing-statement-to-the-court/ (accessed March 1, 2015).

6. The Crackdown and the Chinese Dream

1 Oiwan Lam, "Hundreds arrested for spreading 'rumors' on China's ideological battlefield," Global Voices (website), September 5, 2013. Available at http://advocacy.globalvoicesonline.org/2013/09/05/hundreds-arrested-for-spreading-rumors-on-chinas-ideological-battlefield/ (accessed March 1, 2015).

2 最高人民法院，《最高人民法院、最高人民检察院关于办理利用信息网络实施诽谤等刑事案件适用法律若干问题的解释》，2013年9月5日。 [Supreme People's Court and the Supreme People's Procuratorate, "Interpretation on several questions regarding applicable law when handling the use of information networks to commit defamation and other such criminal cases," September 5, 2013.] Available at http://www.chinacourt.org/law/detail/2013/09/id/146710.shtml (accessed March 1, 2015).

3 David Bandurski, "Rumor fever," *New York Times: Latitude* (blog), December 12, 2011. Available at http://latitude.blogs.nytimes.com/2011/12/12/rumor-fever/?_r=1 (accessed March 1, 2015).

4 Patrick Boehler, "Is anti-rumour crackdown silencing voices of online dissent at Weibo?," *South China Morning Post*, September 13, 2013. Available at http://www.scmp.com/news/china/article/1308860/anti-rumour-crackdown-silencing-voices-online-dissent-weibo (accessed March 1, 2015).

5　《中国互联网络发展状况统计报告》，中国互联网络信息中心，2014年1月。["33rd statistical report on internet development in China," China Internet Network Information Center (website), January 2014.] Available at http://www.cnnic.net.cn/hlwfzyj/hlwxzbg/hlwtjbg/201401/P020140116395418429515.pdf (accessed March 1, 2015).

6　Xuyang Jingjing, "Fall of big V's," *Global Times*, December 17, 2013. Available at http://www.globaltimes.cn/content/832658.shtml#.UrTCQCceeVo (accessed March 1, 2015).

7　Malcolm Moore, "China kills off discussion on Weibo after internet crackdown," *Telegraph*, January 30, 2014. Available at http://www.telegraph.co.uk/news/worldnews/asia/china/10608245/China-kills-off-discussion-on-Weibo-after-internet-crackdown.html (accessed March 1, 2015).

8　Liz Carter, "Don't tweet this Chinese flood," *Foreign Policy*, October 17, 2013. Available at http://www.foreignpolicy.com/articles/2013/10/17/dont_tweet_this_chinese_flood (accessed March 1, 2015).

9　Alia, "Unrest in flooded Chinese city Yuyao over untruthful disaster reporting," *Offbeat China* (blog), October 11, 2013. Available at http://offbeatchina.com/unrest-in-flooded-chinese-city-yuyao-over-untruthful-disaster-reporting (accessed March 1, 2015).

10　Carter, "Don't tweet this Chinese flood."

11　The *Southern Metropolis Daily*'s Weibo post is available at http://www.weibo.com/2105426467/AdgFYAdKI (accessed March 1, 2015).

12　Adam Minter, "China's top Tweeters under fire," Bloomberg (news agency), August 27, 2013. Available at http://www.bloomberg.com/news/2013-08-27/china-s-top-tweeters-under-fire.html (accessed March 1, 2015).

13　"'秦火火'被拘"，《京华时报》，2013年8月21日。["'Qin Huohuo' detained," *Beijing Times*, August 21, 2013.] Available at http://epaper.jinghua.cn/html/2013-08/21/node_100.htm (accessed March 1, 2015).

14　"薛蛮子监狱吐槽：做大V感觉像当皇上　大V薛蛮子的网络心路HD"，YouTube，2015年1月11日。["Big V Xue Manzi's internet journey in HD: Xue Manzi complains from jail: 'Being a Big V was like being an emperor,'" YouTube, January 11, 2015.] Available at https://www.youtube.com/watch?v=JjirArUtous (accessed March 1, 2015).

15　Lilian Lin, "Mother's labor-camp sentence sparks fury," *Wall Street Journal: China Real Time* (blog), August 6, 2012. Available at http://blogs.wsj.com/chinarealtime/2012/08/06/mother%E2%80%99s-labor-camp-sentence-sparks-fury/ (accessed March 1, 2015).

16　周小平，"周小平十问李开复"，《党建网》，2013年10月8日。[Zhou Xiaoping, "Zhou Xiaoping's ten questions for Kai-Fu Lee," Party Building Online, October 8, 2013.] Available at http://dangjian.cn/jrrd/xwmt/201310/t20131008_1506481.shtml (accessed March 1, 2015).

17 Wang Qinglei, "A farewell to CCTV," trans. John, Yaxue Cao, Liz Carter, and Yaqiu Wang, China Change (website), December 9, 2013. Available at http://chinachange.org/2013/12/09/a-farewell-to-cctv/ (accessed March 1, 2015).

18 Ibid.

19 Xin Haiguang, "Rumors and the power of deception," Caixin Online, September 15, 2013. Available at http://english.caixin.com/2013-09-15/100582682.html (accessed March 1, 2015).

20 "Youth urged to contribute to realization of 'Chinese dream,'" Xinhua (news agency), May 4, 2013. Available at http://news.xinhuanet.com/english/china/2013-05/04/c_132359537.htm (accessed March 1, 2015).

21 Tian Ye, "'Mass line' campaign shows CPC's determination," Xinhua (news agency), July 2, 2013. Available at http://news.xinhuanet.com/english/china/2013-07/02/c_132506114.htm (accessed March 1, 2015).

22 Chris Buckley, "China warns officials against 'dangerous' Western values," *New York Times*, May 13, 2013. Available at http://www.nytimes.com/2013/05/14/world/asia/chinese-leaders-warn-of-dangerous-western-values.html?_r=0 (accessed March 1, 2015).

23 Patrick Boehler, "China orders nation's journalists to take Marxism classes," *South China Morning Post*, August 27, 2013. Available at http://www.scmp.com/news/china-insider/article/1299795/china-orders-nations-journalists-take-marxism-classes (accessed March 1, 2015).

24 "250,000 Chinese journalists to receive training," Xinhua (news agency), October 10, 2013. Available at http://news.xinhuanet.com/english/china/2013-10/10/c_132787023.htm (accessed March 1, 2015).

25 Rachel Lu, "Chinese petitioners: here's my 'Chinese dream,'" *Tea Leaf Nation* (website), March 27, 2013. Available at http://www.tealeafnation.com/2013/03/chinese-petitioners-heres-my-chinese-dream/ (accessed March 1, 2015).

26 David Bandurski, "Parsing the 'public opinion struggle,'" China Media Project (website), September 24, 2013. Available at http://cmp.hku.hk/2013/09/24/34085/ (accessed March 1, 2015).

27 Mao Zedong, "On the correct handling of contradictions among the people" [speech at the Eleventh Session (Enlarged) of the Supreme State Conference, February 27, 1957]. Available at http://www.marxists.org/reference/archive/mao/selected-works/volume-5/mswv5_58.htm (accessed March 1, 2015).

28 "网络舆情分析师: 要做的不是删帖", 《新京报》, 2013年10月03日。 ["Internet public opinion analyst: what we need is not post deletion," *Beijing News*, October 3, 2013.] Available at http://epaper.bjnews.com.cn/html/2013-10/03/content_469152.htm?div=-1 (accessed March 1, 2015).

29 Murong Xuecun, "Busting China's bloggers," *New York Times*, October 15, 2013. Available at http://www.nytimes.com/2013/10/16/opinion/murong-busting-chinas-bloggers.html (accessed March 1, 2015).

Recommended Reading

For more about China:

Hessler, Peter, *Country Driving: A Chinese Road Trip* (New York: HarperCollins, 2011).

Hong Fincher, Leta, *Leftover Women: The Resurgence of Gender Inequality in China* (London: Zed Books, 2014).

Lim, Louisa, *The People's Republic of Amnesia: Tiananmen Revisited* (Oxford: Oxford University Press, 2014).

Osnos, Evan, *Age of Ambition: Chasing Fortune, Truth, and Faith in the New China* (New York: Farrar, Straus and Giroux, 2014).

Schell, Orville, and John Delury, *Wealth and Power: China's Long March to the Twenty-first Century* (New York: Random House, 2013).

Wasserstrom, Jeffrey, *China in the 21st Century: What Everyone Needs to Know*, 2nd edition (Oxford: Oxford University Press, 2013).

Yu, Hua, *China in Ten Words*, trans. Allan H. Barr (New York: Vintage, 2011).

And specifically about the internet and censorship in China today:

MacKinnon, Rebecca, *Consent of the Networked: The Worldwide Struggle for Internet Freedom* (New York: Basic Books, 2012).

Ng, Jason Q., *Blocked on Weibo: What Gets Suppressed on China's Version of Twitter (and Why)* (New York: The New Press, 2013).

Parker, Emily, *Now I Know Who My Comrades Are: Voices from the Internet Underground* (New York: Sarah Crichton Books, 2014).

Yang, Guobin, *The Power of the Internet in China: Citizen Activism Online* (New York: Columbia University Press, 2011).

For brevity's sake, the above list is just the tip of the iceberg, including only English-language non-fiction published after 2010 that addresses China specifically. Overlooked books and subject matter should be attributed to gaps in my own reading, not a lack of writing in the field.

There are also other writers whose voices I have come across for the most part online, in articles, essays, and stories they've written and shared. I would recommend these works just as strongly as the books listed above. For in-depth, ground-breaking reporting, read "Billions in hidden riches for family of Chinese leader" by David Barboza (on the *New York Times* website) and "Xi Jinping millionaire relations reveal fortunes of elite" by Michael Forsythe, Shai Oster, Natasha Khan, and Dune Lawrence (on the Bloomberg website). They have tackled the most sensitive of subjects in China and in doing so put their lives and careers on the line. For dogged coverage of China's rights movements, read Yaxue Cao and the contributors of ChinaChange.org. For vulnerable, compelling writing about life in China, I would read everything by Karoline Kan. For insightful long-form journalism on trends in modern China, look up the articles James Palmer has published in the digital magazine *Aeon*. And of course, English-language reporting on China would not be what it is today without David Wertime and Rachel Lu, the founders of *Tea Leaf Nation*, which, in my biased but firmly held opinion, changed everything.

Glossary

50-cent Party – 五毛党 (*wǔ máo dǎng*): A group of people allegedly paid 50 Chinese cents by local- or central-government authorities for each pro-government post made online. The term is broadly used to describe internet commenters whose words seem to toe the Party line or attempt to sway public opinion in favor of the Party.

angry youth – 愤青 (*fèn qīng*): Usually refers to young Chinese who are highly nationalistic, emotional about issues concerning China's territorial sovereignty, and supportive of old-style Communist policies. Their detractors also call them 粪青, an exact homophone that literally translates to "shitty youth."

Big Vs – 大V (*dà vee*): Popular Weibo users whose identities have been verified by the site; they are identifiable by the "V" beside their Weibo handles.

caonima – 草泥马 (*cǎo ní mǎ*): Literally translated as "grass-mud horse" and often depicted as an alpaca, the term is a close homophone for "fuck your mother" – 肏你妈 (*cào nǐ mā*) – and has become a symbol of the anti-censorship movement.

chengguan — 城管 (*chéng guǎn*): Employees of a municipality's City Urban Administrative and Law Enforcement Bureau, who are often assigned unpopular law-enforcement tasks and are perceived to lack effective oversight and training.

danmei — 耽美 (*dān měi*): Literally "aesthetic," the term describes fiction about male homosexual relationships. The characters are pronounced たんび or "*tanbi*" in Japan, where the term originated, likely in the 1970s, as a description of stories about platonic relationships between boys written in very stylized language.

diaosi — 屌丝 (*diǎo sī*): Slang for "loser" often embraced by the "losers" themselves, the term implicitly criticizes the social and economic pressures that make it difficult for young Chinese to attain conventional success.

Food-delivery Party — 送饭党 (*sòng fàn dǎng*): A group of people and organizations who have donated money or services to help the families of imprisoned activists.

fu'erdai — 富二代 (*fù èr dài*): The "wealthy second generation." Young Chinese thought to be spoiled from their upbringing in extravagantly wealthy households. Similar slang exists to describe the offspring of China's government workers — 官二代 (*guān èr dài*): "official second generation" — and the offspring of China's high-profile Communist leaders — 红二代 (*hóng èr dài*): "red second generation."

Great Firewall — 防火长城 (*fáng huǒ cháng chéng*): The massive system of hardware, software, manpower, and bureaucracy that blocks a great amount of online content, including certain websites, within mainland China. Many Chinese internet users refer to it as "GFW" or "the wall" – 墙 (*qiáng*) – and refer to the act of circumventing the Great Firewall as "scaling the wall" – 翻墙 (*fān qiáng*).

human-flesh search – 人肉搜索 (*rén ròu sōu suǒ*): The collective doxing of a person or group of people by a large number of internet users, some of whom may contribute information not publically available online.

invited to tea – 被喝茶 (*bèi hē chá*): More literally "to be tea drinked," the term means to be summoned by police or other authorities due to one's political activities and warned to clean up one's act.

laojiao – 劳教 (*láo jiào*): Short for 劳动教养 (*láo dòng jiào yǎng*), which means "re-education through labor." *Laojiao* was a form of confinement, forced labor, and political education for people whom law-enforcement officers accused of committing minor crimes and political dissidents. Until 2013, when the government abolished the system, law enforcement could imprison people in these labor camps for up to four years without convicting them of crimes.

Lead-the-way Party – 带路党 (*dài lù dǎng*): A term for Chinese who, due to their deep dissatisfaction with the current state of affairs in China, profess that they would "lead the way" in the event of the country being invaded by foreign powers, though this is often more a rhetorical exercise than an earnest self-description.

netizen – 网民 (*wǎng mín*): A portmanteau of "internet" and "citizen," the term is widely used in China to describe an internet user.

the Party – 党 (*dǎng*): Shorthand for the Chinese Communist Party (CCP).

real-name registration – 实名制 (*shí míng zhì*): A policy requiring users of a social-media platform to register their online accounts with their real names or government-issued ID numbers, often as a way to facilitate surveillance and censorship.

Reincarnation Party – 转世党 (*zhuǎn shì dǎng*): A group of people who re-register new social-media accounts after their previous accounts are deleted by internet censors, often due to discussion of sensitive topics.

same-city dinner – 同城饭醉 (*tóng chéng fàn zuì*): A decentralized network of people who gather together regularly over meals to discuss political and social topics. The second half of the phrase, 饭醉, is an exact homophone of 犯罪 – "to commit a crime" – a nod to the somewhat subversive nature of these events.

shangfang – 上访 (*shàng fǎng*): "Petitioning." The act of traveling to the location of an official government building or public location to petition for justice. Today the State Bureau for Letters and Calls is tasked with responding to petitioners, but the practice predates the People's Republic of China by millennia.

shitizen — 屁民 (*pì mín*): A portmanteau of "fart" and "people" (alternatively translated as "fartizen") that describes the kind of second-class-citizen status that many ordinary people feel they have compared to those with wealth and/or political power. The term is often used in self-description and serves as a critique of an existing power structure.

tuhao — 土豪 (*tǔháo*): Literally "dirt splendor," this buzzword describes China's nouveau riche. The term connotes a surplus of money and a lack of taste and tact.

Weibo's "little secretaries" — 微博小秘书 (*wēi bó xiǎo mì shū*): Employees of Sina Weibo tasked with regulating content, often through censorship, on the platform.

weiwen — 维稳 (*wéi wěn*): "Stability maintenance." A loose collection of legal and extra-legal measures, ranging from the detention of dissidents to the compensation of petitioners, intended to maintain social stability.

Index